The C...

Companion Book to the Award-Winning Film
"Please Talk With Me"

By Tim Shaw

Based on Accounts by Key Witnesses to the Events
Chris Di Cesare and J. Jeff Ungar

Please Talk With Me, Directed and Edited by Mara Katria

Copyright © 2012 CITA Ventures
All rights reserved.

Revised Edition – 2016
CITA Productions

ACKNOWLEDGEMENTS

This is not my story. All I did was lend an ear to those who suffered through a very confusing and painful time in their lives. For sharing their stories, I wish to thank Chris Di Cesare, J. Jeff Ungar, Beth Kinsman, and Craig Norris, whose experiences are those that should serve as an example of a deep seated friendship surviving the test of time. I also want to thank Mara Katria, who invited me to attend the first "Please, Talk With Me" symposium held on the campus of the State University of New York at Geneseo, and her production staff, who were most kind to me. I want to thank my little sister, Marla Brooks, who served as my initial editor and whose suggestions were -- and still are -- invaluable. An important contributor was Alan Lewis, who did so much work on the project early on; without his help and insights this book would never have been written. Also, my good friend John Zaffis, who I bombarded with questions, helped me understand that there was more to this story than what everyone had initially thought. I cannot forget my wife Nancy, who would just shake her head when I said that I was driving to Geneseo, NY ... yet again ... to take a couple more photographs, or walk the Geneseo campus. To Paul A., who was Chris's first roommate and who went through so much of the haunting: whether you know it or not, you were important in so many ways. Lastly, I need to thank "Tommy." I hope that in some way you have found the peace you rightfully deserve.

FOREWORD

The world of the *Paranormal* is one that many look at through rose-colored glasses. The wonderment found and the gifts given from the *other side* enlighten the seeker as well as grant fulfillment to the soul. For researchers, it is an exciting and ever-evolving field that promises to push the boundaries of science. However, there are times when the experiences encountered are less than virtuous. For those who stumble upon this type of darkness, the scars of these incidents may run very deep, often lasting a lifetime.

Negative encounters with those entities that dwell in the shadows have become more prevalent in recent years. With the advent of paranormal-based reality television shows, the public at large has become less apprehensive or embarrassed in admitting that they were once the target of a haunting. While most are of a rather mundane variety, there are some which have taken on horrific characteristics that border upon an outright attempt by a spirit personality to possess or influence the life of a living being. While many within the field of the paranormal may debate whether possession is a reality, the fact remains that over the centuries we have read about such experiences; and these types of cases are still being encountered and examined by clergy, the medical community, and educated individuals.

The one reality that I have discovered over the many years that I have done "the work" is that our lives are touched by those who have passed into the ethers. I believe that they are always with us. However, along with those benign spirit personalities, there are negative entities that wish ill upon those who are among the living. It is up to each of us to become aware of the wonders, as well as the pitfalls, of the world that is hidden from our sight.

We must remember that the world of the paranormal surrounds us all. Through research, respect, faith, and the use of common sense, we can become the guideposts for those in need. What better epitaph can any of us leave than that?

John Zaffis

Lecturer, Author, Paranormal Investigator, Demonologist

Stratford, CT, 2012

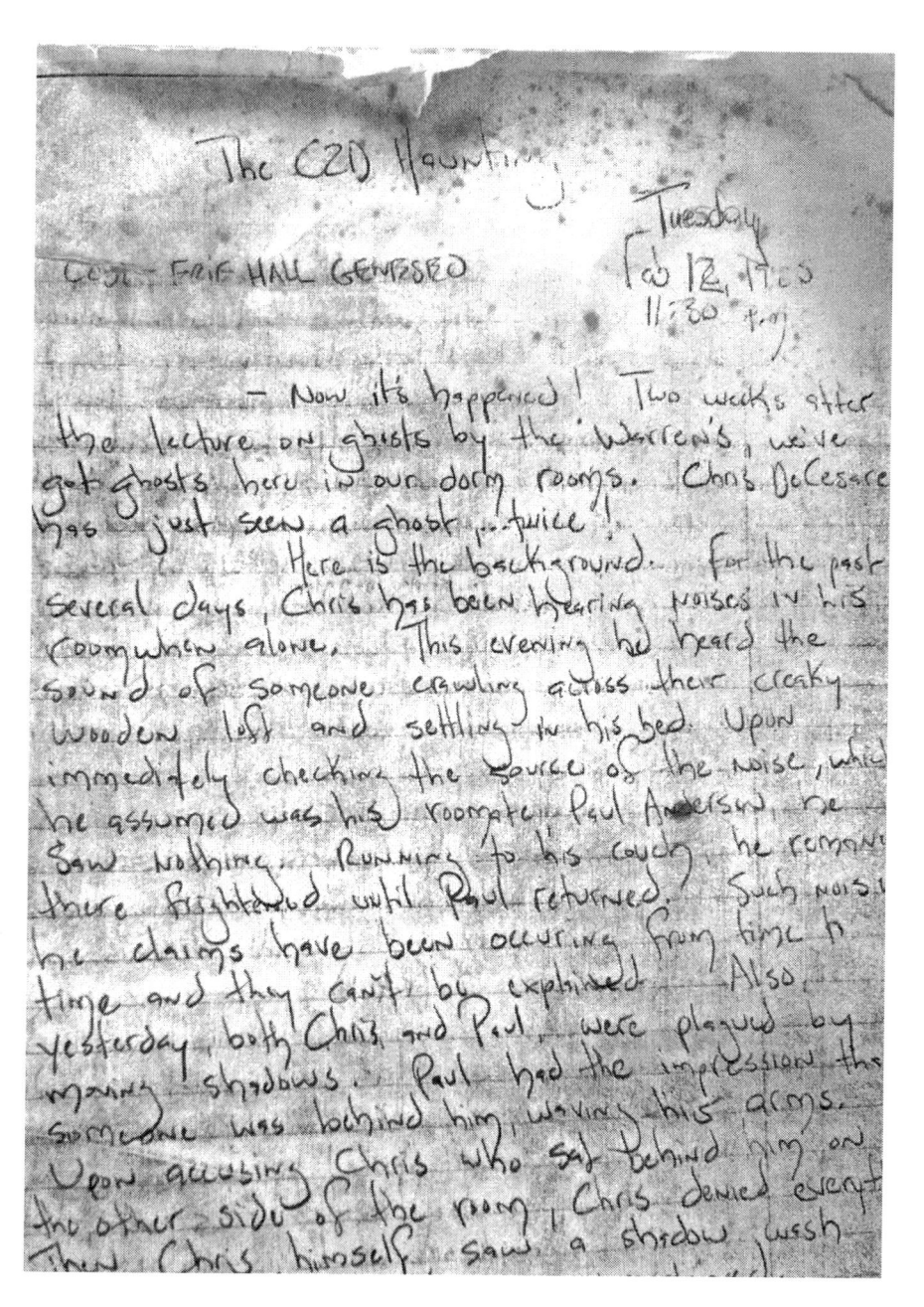

Above: The C2D(1) Journal Notes, as recorded by J. Jeff Ungar in 1985.

INDEX

Foreword

Acknowledgments

Chapter One :	Urban Legends	1
Chapter Two :	A Bloody And Superstitious Land: (Livingston County, New York)	5
Chapter Three :	A Runner's Life	15
Chapter Four :	Erie Hall	23
Chapter Five :	The Beginning Of A Friendship	28
Chapter Six :	The Warrens	35
Chapter Seven :	I Heard Someone Call My Name	41
Chapter Eight :	It's Looking At Me	53
Chapter Nine :	Now I Lay Me Down To Sleep	61
Chapter Ten :	What To Do?	71
Chapter Eleven :	A Single Candle In The Dark	79
Chapter Twelve :	The Bleak And Dreary Winter	83
Chapter Thirteen :	The Oppressed	89
Chapter Fourteen :	Deliver Me From Evil	95
Chapter Fifteen :	Enter The Whirlwind	105

Chapter Sixteen :	When the Dead Come Calling	111
Chapter Seventeen :	A Father's Love	117
Chapter Eighteen :	Proof At Last	127
Chapter Nineteen :	The Confrontation	135
Chapter Twenty :	The World Today	143
The Survivors		145
Bibliography		151
About the Author		152
Additional Information		155

1. URBAN LEGENDS

Webster's Dictionary defines an Urban Legend as: "A story, which may have started with a grain of truth, that has been embroidered and retold until it has passed into the realm of myth." This type of mythology is an interesting phenomenon, as these stories seem to gather their own momentum and are spread so far, so fast, by so many. These legends in ancient times once served as moral and cautionary tales, harkening back to a time when ancient man lived in small tribal bands fighting for survival. In modern times, the Urban Legend has morphed to include subjects of macabre interest, rather than ancient codes of conduct. Generation after generation now hands down stories of monsters and ghouls for the expressed thrill and goose bumps that they may produce. This is exactly what happened to the actual events of the haunting of a dorm room located on the State University of New York at Geneseo's campus in 1985.

The story of the "C2D1 Haunting of Erie Hall" is a complicated one. On the surface it may look to be something that might be easy to understand -- it happened; it was scary; people survived it and pretty much went on with their lives. Unfortunately, as in most cases of violent hauntings, there is so much more to the story. Each haunting in and of itself is unique in its own way. To understand what the targeted individual has gone through, the researcher must not only listen to witness accounts, but also delve beneath the surface in the attempt to figure out the "who, what, when, where, and whys" of the case. It is only when these concepts are properly addressed that the truth can be exposed to the world.

The C2D1 legend is about a student who became targeted by the mysterious and quite mischievous spirit of a young man. This ghost not only appeared to him, but also violently attacked him. For many years, paranormal enthusiasts have attempted to track down the key facts of this story, often visiting the Geneseo campus in order to interview anyone with knowledge of the actual incidents. Unfortunately, most came up empty-handed, as the late 1980s through the early years of 2000 were not conducive to this type of study.

The "post-Reagan" era had relegated the paranormal to abstract or religious thought. The chaos of world events came crashing down, and society struggled to keep bread on the table and lead "normal" lives. This all changed when on October 6th, 2004, the SiFi Channel (now SyFy) would broadcast what has become a cultural phenomenon: the television show *Ghost Hunters* was premiered, and in its wake, revolutionized how the American public viewed the concept of life-after-death.

At the time of the actual haunting in 1985, the witnesses felt that society would think of them as "odd" if they told their stories. However, after the 2004 premiere of *Ghost Hunters*, it became apparent that the majority of our society not only *accepted* the concept of the paranormal as being (paradoxically-speaking) almost commonplace, but most could boast of encountering something supernatural *themselves.*

For those stalwart researchers of the haunting of the C2D1 Erie Hall dorm quad at Geneseo State, the modern boon in paranormal awareness pushed back the veil of mystery that had shrouded this story. In July of 2011, a man bravely stepped forward to announce that not only was the legend true, but that he himself was, in fact, the student who had experienced the violent haunting of his dorm room those many years ago. Having relegated this painful episode to the past, and having built a successful life for himself and his family, he felt that the time was now right to begin talking of his experience; the stigma of being known as the "Ghost Boy" was no longer something to be feared. It is his wish now not only to share his story, but to let those who may have suffered through a violent haunting themselves know that they are not alone.

Above – The window of room C2D1, the epicenter of the C2D1 haunting.

In order to come to some conclusion about the mystery of the C2D1 Haunting, a number of factors needed to be addressed. The early history of Geneseo and its environs was researched to ascertain if there might be any possible links to the haunting. Various metaphysical theories had to be taken into consideration, as the paranormal often does not act in a logical fashion and will defy the practice of the scientific method. Lastly, multiple eye-witness accounts were collected and carefully examined, both to rule out fraud and faulty memories and to seek corroborative evidence.

Finally, whenever we deal with a project such as the C2D1 Haunting, researchers should be aware that, regardless of the miles of paper trails that are followed, the number of witnesses interviewed, and the travel endured to closely examine the actual locations of the incidents, each legend and story speaks to us of the human experience. It is not just a literary endeavor, but truly an adventure of the mind, as well as of the soul: respect is paramount.

2. A BLOODY AND SUPERSTITIOUS LAND
(GENESEO, LIVINGSTON COUNTY, NEW YORK)

Today, people enjoy strolling along Geneseo's shop-lined Main Street, where they can look at antiques or stop for a cup of coffee at a local cafe. The neighborhood itself possesses a certain charm left over from a bygone age. Elegantly restored Victorian and cobblestone homes, art galleries and shops are all within easy walking distance from one of the most highly acclaimed academic facilities in the Northeast -- The State University of New York at Geneseo.

Geneseo is located in Livingston County, an area nestled quietly within the Finger Lakes region of New York, which is well-known as a vacation destination that boasts of idyllic lakes, breathtaking scenery, and award winning wineries. Formed by ancient glaciers, the casual visitor and tourist alike will discover that a beautiful vista of pastoral farmlands, gentle valleys, and lazy rivers awaits them. However, below the surface of this seeming depiction of heaven-on-earth, lies an undercurrent of death, suffering, and mystery that bubbles to the surface when conditions are just right.

The Village of Geneseo was founded in 1789, and its name was taken from the original Native American word "Gen-nis-he-yo," which, roughly translated, means "beautiful valley." Located directly upon the sites of former Native American settlements-- most notably "Big Tree" and "Casaseraga" -- many war Pre-European Contact Period stone tools and other artifacts have been found. As a result of the need for more farmland and pressure from residential and industrial development, several burial mounds are known to have been disturbed during the clearing and leveling of the forests, and the construction of buildings and industrial railroad spurs.

The early native inhabitants using stone implements hacked a life from the wilderness -- not only merely surviving, but flourishing with a unique culture -- establishing great centers of trade and commerce. Found during archeological digs were objects brought to the region by a great network of ancient trade routes: red pipestone from Minnesota; grayish-black chert mined in the Mohawk Valley of New York State from which the strongest arrow heads and knives were fashioned; even a tooth or two of the Great White Shark from the Florida Gulf. These ancient people may have seemed primitive by our modern standards, but they were far more advanced in travel and commerce than the first Europeans who explored the Great Lakes region gave them credit for.

The earliest recorded inhabitants of this great land were the "Onondowahgah," roughly translated as the "People of the Great Hill" (Seneca to the whites who established trade posts in the 1600s.) Seneca lands stretched from the Allegheny River in the south, up passed the Genesee River to approximately Canandaigua Lake in Western New York. Joining four other Indian nations around the year 1142 AD, they helped create the "Haudensaunee," which means, "They Are Building A Long House," or what is referred to today as the "Iroquois Confederacy." The reason for the formation of this league of Native American nations was to seek more productive hunting lands and for intertribal harmony. Initially referred to as the "Five Nations" to the Europeans who were colonizing the Great Lakes area, they officially became the "Six Nations" after the migration from North Carolina of the Tuscarora's in the early 18th century. After the formation of the Iroquois Confederacy, the Seneca People were given the name, "The Keepers of the Western Door," signifying that they lived and protected the western border lands of the Iroquois.

Once all of the tribes had joined together, this single nation became a mighty force to reckon with. It was symbolized by a bundle of arrows, which taught that while a single arrow shaft could easily be bent or shattered by enemy hands, a bundle of arrows could not be so easily broken. This became a hard-learned lesson that other tribes, as well as European colonial nations, would discover.

In the early 1600s, a new fad swept continental Europe: hats made of the skin of beavers found in American waterways became a highly desired commodity. (The skins were tanned with a mercury compound which was highly poisonous. Symptoms included erratic movement and speech, which caused people to coin the phrase, "mad as a hatter".) During this time period, more hunting and trapping areas were aggressively sought after, and the Iroquois decided to take to the warpath against their traditional enemies, the Erie and Kah-Kwas, better known as the Neutral Nation. Many battles were fought and these two ancient peoples were either conquered and assimilated into the Seneca/Iroquois Confederacy or exterminated altogether. Their lands became Iroquois territory.

It was for this reason that the Keepers of the Western Door were courted by foreign ambassadors wishing to ally themselves with such a powerful aboriginal tribe. Early on, they traded with the French and ceded land to them, which established white trade routes along the Great Lakes and into the continent's interior.

During the American Revolutionary War, most of the tribes of the Iroquois had allied themselves with Great Britain. In return for plunder, they took part in depredations against the outlying farms and villages loyal to the revolutionary government.

This caused General George Washington to send a force under Major General John Sullivan to destroy the homeland of the Iroquois, crush its legion of warriors, deprive the British of sustenance and force the Native populace to rely on supply depots on the Great Lakes. This, it was hoped, would overtax British supply depots, especially during the harsh winter months. The punitive expedition set out on June 18th, 1779, from Easton, Pennsylvania, and headed north, destroying all the Indian farmlands, orchards, and villages that they encountered. Several pitched battles ensued; however, the American war machine was almost unstoppable.

Sullivan's forces reached the furthest point in their campaign when they overtook the Seneca town of "Chenussio" -- also called "Little Beard's Town" after the war chief who lived there. (The actual location is just a stone's throw from the college campus in Geneseo, near what is now Cuylerville, N.Y.)

When the soldiers began the systematic destruction of the surrounding crops and buildings, they were horrified to discover the mutilated remains of two white captives. Lieutenant Thomas Boyd and Sergeant Michael Parker had been part of an advanced scouting party that was probing enemy lines. On September 13^{th,} 1779, Lieutenant Boyd's small detachment was ambushed by Native warriors. All of the members of the scouting party were killed except for Boyd and Parker who survived only to be tortured and killed later on. When Sullivan's soldiers reached the abandoned town, they found their horribly mutilated bodies near what is called "The Torture Tree." The aftermath of Sullivan's "scorched earth" campaign was the destruction of the power base of the Iroquois people and their forcible internment on government-issued reservations following the war. Suffering such defeat, Seneca mothers were known to quiet their crying children by saying, "Hush, Town Burner is near"-- "Town Burner" being the nickname that the Seneca gave to George Washington following this controversial military operation.

Above – The current day "Torture Tree" site near Rt. 20A in Geneseo, NY

Aboriginal Tales Of Monsters And Witchcraft

As in all Native American mythology, there is an abundance of things that go bump in the night. The Seneca Nation (as well as the other tribes of the mighty Iroquois) are steeped in curious legends and horrific customs. Many of these stories and customs can be found to still scar this region's landscape. One such legend was that of the Flying Head. This creature was known to invade the homes of Native people after dark and devour them. It was described as possessing the features of a man attached to the legs of what might be referred to as a mountain lion. The only defense that the people had was to fortify their individual living spaces or to keep a fire lit. It was said that an elderly woman was parching acorns one evening when a Flying Head appeared. It entered her lodge; but once having observed the fire, it screamed with fear and sank into the earth, taking with it many other of these dreaded monsters.

Another dire beast was a great serpent that wandered the paths that led from the Genesee River to Canandaigua Lake. It was known to attack villages and consume any unwary traveler it happened upon. Indian lore tells of a young man who found a small snake that possessed a human head. He took it home and fed it the flesh of a bird. As it grew to monstrous proportions, so did its appetite. Eventually, it began to stalk the trails that connected the Indian towns, devouring anything that was made of flesh. A group of young braves was chosen, and after a pitched battle, the snake was slain.

Also found in the rich mythology of these people was a race of Stone Giants that was rumored to have originated far beyond the Mississippi River. Their bodies were covered with sand and gravel which made them safe from the blows of arrows. They ravaged the land and destroyed many towns until the deity "Holder of the Heavens" returned to the Earth. He tricked these giants into entering a great cavern; and when they fell asleep, he caused boulders to rain down upon them, killing them.

When we think of witchcraft, we often visualize black robed individuals with pointy hats that rule the world on All Hallows' Eve. We might also associate it with the Spanish Inquisition in Europe, or with the hysteria surrounding the Salem Witch Trials in North America. However, the 'People of the Great Hill' also possessed an impressive tradition of witchcraft. In fact, any death, with the exception of an obvious accident or death by warfare, could be attributed to the work of sorcery. During these early time periods, there was much in the world that was not readily understood. The causes of miraculous interventions as well as terrible misfortunes were often ascribed to external influences, which in some circumstances, were witches.

In Lockwood Doty's "History of Livingston" (compiled in 1876) we find the following quote:

> *The notions of our forefathers, in common with their generation, (Both Native American as well as White settlers) were tinged with that superstition which credit's the existence of a race of supernatural beings peopling the recesses of forests; of which witches who haunted those persons who their capricious natures led them to annoy or who, gypsy like, told fortunes, made and dissolved matches, interfered with household affairs, and discovered stolen property. Omens, too were observed, dreams were not unheeded, and many a farmer plowed, planted, and gathered, according to aspects of the moon, while few domesticated animals were held as free from direct planetary influences.*

Of Pain And Cannibalism

When we research the early culture of many indigenous peoples, we often find in their deep, dark past, instances of ritualistic torture, and sometimes cannibalism. Here on the North American continent, we don't always associate some of these horrific deeds with those of "Indigenous People." Research into the traditions of the Iroquois tribes can often find examples of these activities. Torture was, in truth, universally accepted by the members of the Iroquois Confederacy.
In Dean Snow's work "The Iroquois," he writes:

> *Torture took many forms, beginning with the removal of fingernails so the captive could not easily untie his bindings.*

Prisoners who survived the journey back to an Iroquois village were forced to run a gauntlet in which everyone, even small children were allowed to strike or stab at the prisoner. If the prisoner was marked for death, (s)he would often be placed on a scaffold and tortured by a variety of means. Red-hot iron axes were hung as a necklace on the prisoner; fingers were burned or cut off. A prisoner might be forced to eat his own flesh. Resolute prisoners clung to their dignity, singing their death songs in the face of excruciating pain until they lost consciousness. Occasionally they would be revived so that the torture could continue, but once their condition became grave they were killed. Children were anointed with the blood of the brave victims, and warriors consumed their hearts, all so that they might acquire a portion of the victim's courage. More extensive cannibalism sometimes followed."

The Feast of the Dead

To early Jesuit missionaries, many of the Seneca and Iroquois customs seemed barbaric and disgusting. In a seminal work, *The Jesuit Relations*, which chronicles Jesuit exploits in the North

American wilderness, is found a description of one of the most sacred ceremonies of Iroquois culture, "The Feast of the Dead."

Dean Snow again shares with us an account of this fascinating mortuary ritual:

> *Members of the opposite moiety arranged things for the bereaved. The deceased was dressed in traditional clothing, his or her "dead clothes". The longhouse was cleaned. Mirrors and other things that might reflect images were covered lest anyone (especially children) be frightened by seeing the ghost in them. Food was set out for the deceased, and at least two people stayed with the body. A wake was held the night before the funeral, at which the moccasin or a dice game was played.*

He also relates the following about the soul:

> *The soul of the deceased was thought to linger, not leaving until the Tenth Day Feast was held. The possessions of the deceased that were not to be buried were distributed. The feast itself featured the favorite foods of the deceased. Once this took place, the soul could travel along the Milky Way, the Path of Souls. A year later another feast was held for the deceased, and this marked the end of a year of mourning. No doubt much of this ceremonial was dropped during episodes of widespread mortality.*

> *Once or twice a year there was traditionally a general Feast of the Dead. This featured a speech, tobacco invocation, songs, and a dance. Iroquois dancers almost always proceed counterclockwise. However, in this case the dancing was often clockwise, and the dead were believed to join the living in dancing. Food was served after midnight, and there were often presents, especially cloth. It was important on the death*

on an individual to redistribute clothing, and the custom was continued during the Feast of the Dead.

Why research monsters, witches and flesh eaters when working on a case involving the paranormal? It gives the researcher a cultural and historical account of the inhabitants who once lived on the very land where the modern town of Geneseo is now located. They will discover that the land was once ruled by superstitions and the emotions of fierce warfare and death may have left a bloody impact on the geology of the region.

It is commonly believed in some metaphysical circles there are areas that may have "residual imprints" of events that took place many years ago. Could this explain why some locations are hotbeds of paranormal activity centuries after something traumatic took place? As in forensic studies, "the past is just a stepping stone to understanding the present."

3. A RUNNER'S LIFE

The fall semester of 1984 at the State University of New York at Geneseo began like every previous semester had: students could be found orientating themselves to the campus grounds; visiting the bookstore for required course materials; hanging out at the Student Union; and catching up with friends they hadn't seen all summer. The cooler weather was pleasant enough as the hills surrounding the campus began to come alive with early Autumn colors. *So many things to do, so many possibilities for the future,* Chris thought to himself as he excitedly contemplated the upcoming school year. He was a member of the University's cross country and track running teams, and while he surveyed the surrounding country roads, he thought with great satisfaction that this could quite possibly be his breakout year. Also, like many politically aware students of the early 80s, he felt that he was part of some "great cohesive social understanding" which was both refreshing and exciting. President Ronald Reagan -- an early role model for Chris -- was running for his second term in office and there was a feeling on campus that he would protect them from the "Evil Empire" (U.S.S.R) and that somehow "Reaganomics" would stimulate a sagging U.S. economy.

Chris' father, Vito Di Cesare, was the first person in his family to graduate from college. He was a man born of logic and hard learned common sense. A teacher of biology, chemistry and physics when Chris was a small child, he later became a school principal. As such, Mr. Di Cesare espoused the theories of the German philosopher Immanuel Kant. Kant had theorized that scientific knowledge, morality and religious belief could be equally unswerving and secure as they all rest on the same foundation of human autonomy. Thus most things in life could be verifiable through observation and experimentation. Vito was a warm, outspoken but 'no nonsense' type of guy. He could see the endless possibilities in his son -- a child who enjoyed making star charts and reading comic books; but he decided that it would be through physical education that Chris might best begin to realize the potential he possessed, that is ... if he could ever get Chris to leave his room and go outside into the fresh air.

Running was something that Vito strongly encouraged Chris to do. In fact, when Chris was eleven Mr. Di Cesare announced a new rule, "If you don't run, you don't eat." And since Chris loved to eat -- he obeyed his father's instructions. They began to jog together on a regular basis, Vito urging his son on. It is ironic, however, that Chris did not like to run -- he did it simply to please his father;

and he would sometimes attempt to break free from the routine. On one particular run, Chris got tired and wanted to stop; so he pretended to injure his knee. Vito looked at him sternly and asked, "Are you lying to me?" To which Chris, unable to maintain the deception, sheepishly replied, "...yes." At that, Vito grabbed a switch from a nearby tree and chased the young Chris for almost three miles. Distraught by the perceived abuse of his 'forced' run, Chris -- who was still in grammar school at the time -- threatened to call the police. Unmoved, his father calmly said, "Look at your watch." When Chris grudgingly complied, he was amazed to see that he had run the three miles in eighteen minutes and forty seconds, a time he knew from his reading that only high school runners were supposed to be capable of achieving. That was when Chris realized he had a genuine talent for running; and that perhaps he could even do something great with it someday.

The actual pursuit of running would not only win Chris accolades and a shelf-full of trophies, but also help build in him a healthy self-esteem. Distance running became so important in his life that he adopted as his motto a quote from the Japanese world-class Marathon runner, Toshihiko Seko, who said, "The marathon is my only girlfriend. I give her everything I have." Eventually, Chris would compete in several 26.2 mile marathons himself. His first would be the Montreal International Marathon which he entered the summer after 8th grade. His goal was to break the four hour barrier, which he promptly did. And aside from being the hungriest he had "ever been" afterwards, he felt no ill effects. This only served to inspire him more.

Young Chris soon became a "runner's runner" -- with every breath he took, his focus remained completely on his ultimate goal: becoming a member of the U.S. Olympic Track Team. There seemed to be a great pride that swept not only his hometown but the nation itself during this time period. The Los Angeles Summer

Olympics had been held the previous year, and everywhere you looked there were reminders of that glorious event. T-Shirts bearing patriotic symbols and hats with flag emblems on them seemed to have become the national dress code. It was as if the 'United States' for a brief -- and rare -- moment in time had become united in the pride that such an event brings.

Above – Chris Di Cesare, age 17, completing a 13.1 mile half-marathon race.

After graduating from Valley Central High School in Montgomery, N.Y., Chris began to search for a college that would offer what he needed academically, as well as athletically. After an exhaustive search, he eventually decided to attend the State University of New York at Geneseo. The university was originally founded as the Wadsworth Normal and Training School in 1871, and became a state-affiliated liberal arts college in 1948. The town that surrounded the college greatly appealed to him with its old buildings and a landscape that was perfect for long distance runners.

Another important aspect in making his decision was that if he was to take the three-year Baccalaureate Exam and achieve a score of 90 or better, the university would give him credit for the entire first year for free. This program enabled students to enroll as sophomores instead of freshmen and finish their degrees in an accelerated three years of study. Knowing that other educational institutions gave full scholarships to those taking part in their athletic programs, Chris made the decision to not accept them. He felt that the financial risk was too great. If he attended such a school, he would be required to dedicate himself 100% to the sport of running, which was fine. But while this might have been an acceptable dream to others, Chris recognized that if he ever were to become injured and unable to compete, he might very well lose everything that he had worked so hard for -- including a higher education.

Above – Di Cesare, center, with the 1985 Geneseo Cross Country Team.

Geneseo offered him a place where he could not only run without all the external pressures associated with the other schools, but where he could also train under Martin Kentner, a coach that he greatly admired.

Arriving on campus, Chris experienced a sort of culture shock watching with great interest the way in which students interacted.

He often contemplated on how being a part of college life was akin to observing some great experiment, going to a zoo or being on a wild safari. When time allowed, he would sit by himself on a bench outside his dorm and be amazed at what other students were doing and how they were dressed. To a kid from a conservative family this was as alien to him as the landscape of Mars. Even things that many students took for granted seemed to really amaze Chris. It was an age when MTV dominated the airwaves, and all such programming had been frowned upon at home.

Above – Di Cesare wearing his National Cross Country Championship t-shirt.

He was exposed for the first time to music videos and would wait eagerly each Friday night to watch such artists as the Eurythmics, The Police, Adam Ant, and Genesis perform. To Chris, this was a profound form of freedom that exposed him to a new world of experience and thought.

He also lacked for the very first time that familiar structure of life that he was so used to. Now, there was no one around him who would advise him when to get up, what to eat, or when to go to bed. Without such a core element, Chris suddenly realized just how large the world actually was and that so much was happening around him. With eyes now opened, Chris saw that there was so much more to life than he ever before realized. Some of it worried him.

Young Chris had trained hard to begin his quest for Olympic Glory. Being a runner was in his blood, and as such, he would focus his body and mind on achieving this goal. He would often sit alone in his dorm room and ponder what he needed to do next in order to push himself to that next level.

Above – Running laps on the indoor track above Geneseo's indoor ice rink.

In Chris' mind it was never a question of whether or not he could accomplish something. But rather how he would change his routine in order to achieve a particular goal. Chris understood most of the lessons that his father tried to teach him, and he knew that his extreme focus was not just born of his need for athletic perfection, but also from a deep-set morality that had been instilled in him from childhood.

Life on the Geneseo campus seemed to exude the promise of a new day and never-ending adventure. However, none of us can truly see what lies in our future. For many, nothing that we may already take for granted can prepare us for the challenges that might randomly enter our lives.

Fall Semester, 1984, would become the pleasant prelude to the horrific ordeal that Chris would experience the following semester.

4. ERIE HALL

Built to serve the needs of residential students, Erie Hall is a classic box design consisting of three square buildings, three stories high, that are interconnected by enclosed walkways. At first glance, other than its red brick and tan stone facade and symmetrically placed windows, the casual observer would ascertain that its purpose was more about functionality than actual comfort. This assumption is proven incorrect upon closer inspection. The "C" building's second and third floors are divided into common and semi-private living spaces. "Quads," as each floor is known, are comprised of four living suites, each divided into three or four bedrooms, a bath, and a common living area. The bedrooms are spacious enough to meet the needs of two students easily.

Originally, in 1983, Chris shared a room with a senior classman in another building. The young-looking Chris recalls being continuously hazed by him: buckets of ice were tossed on him as he showered; his bed was short sheeted; and Chris became the target of all sorts of practical jokes. It was then that he decided he needed to look for someone new to bunk with. Chris met his future roommate Paul in the dining hall after a run at the campus athletic center. Paul was also an athlete who played lacrosse and soccer. Most importantly, he seemed to be a decent, clean-cut and honest guy. The two hit it off and agreed to share a room the following semester; and just to make sure that they were compatible enough to live together, each took a trip to visit the other's family, and they corresponded with each other regularly over the summer.

Chris looked forward to dorm-rooming with Paul because he felt that as an athlete, he would follow the lifestyle of one. So alike were the two in stature (both standing at 5'6" and weighing 130 lbs.) that those sharing the C2D suite would eventually take to calling them "The Twins." Paul, with his matching brown eyes and hair was the labeled the 'Dark Twin' while Chris, being blue-eyed and blond was referred to as the 'Light Twin'. However, that was where most of the similarities ended.

Paul seemed certain that Chris was a ladies' man. But this perception wasn't exactly true. Chris was always friendly and respectful around girls -- sometimes even innocently being pulled into a bubble bath shower fight with them -- and he mistakenly gave Paul the impression that he was a 'player.' The truth of the matter was that at that early stage of his life he preferred simply being a girl's friend rather than pursuing a serious relationship. In reality, it was Paul who was more interested in 'experiencing life' like most their age. Chris was more of a self-described hermitic monk, greatly focused upon his studies and running.

Above – Chris Di Cesare and his roommate Paul A in room C2D1.

Expectations were high when the two of them moved into Erie Hall on September 3rd, 1984. As previously mentioned, the complex is composed of three individual buildings. The actual dormitory that Chris and Paul moved into was the "C" dorm which was oddly located *between* the A and B buildings. The room they were to occupy was on the second floor in suite "D." It was the first one to be found on the right, closest to the suite's main door, thus the room's designation: "C2D1." A large window with a view of a maple tree outside it dominated the far wall of the common living area directly opposite the suite's outer door.

Ironically, the dorm's Resident Assistant had chosen a 'welcome back' theme for Chris' floor which he'd taken from the hit movie *Ghostbusters* that had been popular that summer: when he and Paul arrived, they found the iconic *Ghostbusters* logo prominently attached to their door at eye-level. Chris immediately expressed his displeasure at the choice, as he thought the movie was "really dumb."

To maximize the space available, Paul's family had purchased a wooden loft which Chris described as "a sort of tree house" made of a plywood platform approximately 5 feet from the ground on which they placed their mattresses.

Above – Di Cesare sitting at his desk, under the loft, in room C2D1, Erie Hall.

Paul occupied the left corner and Chris the right corner, with ladder rungs for access at the foot of each. Underneath the sleeping areas they hung netting which held shells and starfish over a couch and stereo system. They decorated the rest of the room with Christmas lights and posters, which seemed to make it the perfect college dorm bachelor pad. Eventually, Chris and Paul would meet the rest of their suitemates.

Being so dedicated to his running, Chris did not leave himself much time for extracurricular activities. He did run for a spot on the dorm council but quickly realized that he lacked the time to properly dedicate himself to the job after he won the race. The previous year he had served as the illustration editor for the school newspaper, *The Lamron*; but there too, he had felt that he did not have the time to do the required layouts and comic strips. His goal of becoming a world-class competitor was an all-consuming one, and if he was to accomplish this goal, he realized that he would have to dedicate every extra minute that he had to training.

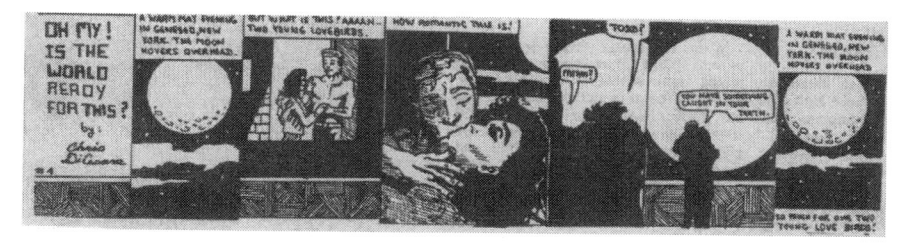

Above – One of three comic strip series that Di Cesare created for the paper.

After a short time, the two roommates began to experience a few small adjustment issues that would in time become chronic. Chris' self-imposed schedule was extremely regimented. He arose at 5:45 A.M. in order to run till 7:00 A.M.. Next, he would return to his dorm room for a quick shower, dress quickly, and attend a full day of academic classes. Around 2:00 P.M., he would change back into his workout clothing and attend the university's official cross country practice, and afterwards eat dinner around 4:30 P.M..

Paul, on the other hand, enjoyed the college social scene, opting to go out for a couple of beers and stay up late. Eventually, these differences would have a detrimental effect on their once rock-solid friendship. The roommates, still known as The Twins, would see their relationship go from best friends to merely friends in several short months.

5. THE BEGINNING OF A FRIENDSHIP

It was at a dorm party shortly after the semester had begun that someone asked the baby-faced Chris what his story was. When Chris replied that he was a sophomore, they began to mock him, saying, "What are you, like twelve years old?" Others joined in, stating with certainty that he was "too young and didn't belong with them." At that moment, a bearded student with wire-rim glasses piped up and said, "No, it's true. He's actually a three-year student like myself. I can vouch for him! I saw his name on the list." Jeff Ungar had recognized Chris as someone who did indeed share the C2D suite and who had something else in common with himself: intelligence. He could also see that Chris was in need of a friend.

Many of the students in the dorm considered Jeff to be highly intelligent as well as "odd and very eccentric." He was someone who was always watching and observing the world around him.

He was never without a notebook or his 35mm camera. Jeff was the son of a well-known local architect and had graduated with honors from R. L. Thomas High School in Webster, N.Y. Finding the world around him so curious as a child, he would venture on "excursions" where he would look for fossils, arrowheads, rocks and old bottles of every type. Jeff considered himself to be a student of human nature. He watched how the pecking order …

STATE UNIVERSITY COLLEGE OF ARTS AND SCIENCE, GENESEO, N.Y. 14454

EDUCATIONAL SERVICES
ORIENTATION PROGRAM
BEGINNINGS 1983

Wadsworth Auditorium
3:00 - 3:30 pm.

I have just received your card indicating that you are coming to orientation and are interested in taking the three year degree examinations offered on June 30. The Educational Testing Service provides the examinations, which last for about an hour each. The three general areas involved are natural science, social science, and fine arts. A fee of $12 will be charged at the door for test administration and scoring.

Because the three year tests are an addition to the regular orientation program which begins at 3:30 p.m., you must arrive at Ontario Hall between 9:00 a.m. and 11:30 a.m. on June 30. The three year tests will begin promptly at 12:00 noon in the Newton Lecture Hall, Room 202.

If you live more than five hours from campus, we can allow you to check into Ontario Hall between 7:00 - 10:00 p.m. the night before your scheduled date. If you are interested in this option, please call (716) 245-5717 as soon as possible, but no later than June 22, 1983. There will be no additional cost for this arrangement. If either or both of your parents will be accompanying you, they too, will be accommodated. Please remember to bring your own linen and blanket.

We are really pleased with the quality of this year's Freshman Class and look forward to meeting you at orientation.

Sincerely,

Dr. James L. Allan
Director of Orientation

Above – Information on the three year exam that both Chris and Jeff took.

... manifested itself in Erie Hall and would not stand for the high school drama and pack mentality that some students brought with them from home. It was because he was so often viewed by others as being "intense" that other students would listen and take note when he spoke.

Jeff thought to himself that Chris seemed to be a good person worth sticking up for. He described Chris as "frenetic" -- someone who had more to him that met the eye. Chris, meanwhile, was continuously grateful to Jeff for having come to his aid. It seemed only natural that they would become good friends.

Above – J. Jeff Ungar, with his trusty 35mm camera, photographs Di Cesare during a 10K foot race on the SUNY Geneseo campus in 1985.

Chris soon noticed, and became quite amused by one of Jeff's eccentricities. While he was extremely inquisitive and never shied away from asking a question, he was painfully awkward around members of the opposite sex. He often would call them by the generic name "people" or "persons" whenever referring to them. He would say, "I saw Paul with some people," when in fact he had seen Paul with a group of girls. Or "I spoke with some person in my class today."

Chris thought to himself: *If this is as bad as it gets, I can live with it.* Besides, since arriving at college he found that he was often surrounded by girls seeking his affection. And, being around Jeff might offer the potential for some extremely humorous entertainment as well.

As the semester began to get into full swing, Chris slowly acclimated himself to his new dorm mates and began to make friends. Once, when asked to describe Jeff, a quote borrowed from Jane Austen's novel *Pride and Prejudice* aptly fit: "The power of doing anything with quickness is always prized much by the possessor, and often without any attention to the imperfection of the performance."

To Jeff, being observant was the key to all things in life.

Along with those on his track team, Chris most often could be seen hanging out with Jeff and fellow Geneseo students Beth Kinsman, Judy Y., Linda Fox, and Jeff's friend, Craig Norris. Together they formed a small but close-knit family. This greatly helped all of them ease the anxiety of being away from home and the increased work load that a higher education demands.

For them and the other students of Erie Hall in January of 1985, the mundane grind of campus life was interspersed with the excitement that only a dorm party could bring. The most famous of all college "theme parties" was, of course, the one that has been emulated on college campuses all over the world -- the "Toga Party."

Above – Scenes from the January 1985 Erie Hall Toga Party. Di Cesare (bottom left), Ungar (bottom right) and friend Craig Norris (top right).

Based on the cult-classic film *Animal House*, participants would wrap bed sheets on themselves and wallow in bacchanalian debauchery (or as debauched as could be gotten away with on campus before college security was called in.) The sheet clad revelers laughed, drank beer, and danced the night away listening to the strains of Pat Benatar, Cyndi Lauper, and Frankie Goes to Hollywood. Jeff, with camera in hand, recorded many of the silly antics that had gone on that evening. Eventually, he passed his camera to another student and jumped into a photo with Chris and his other fellow C2D suitemates. Jeff thought to himself that this would be one of those happy moments destined to become frozen in time. It would be something to look back on, something that would jog the memory when they had all graduated and gone on to successful lives. What he could not possibly take into account was that it would also signal a change in all of their lives. Never again would they be able to look at the world through childlike eyes.

On the evening of January 30, 1985, Paul was attempting to convince Chris to accompany him and several young ladies to go dancing. Knowing that the rift between 'The Twins' was beginning to widen, Jeff offered up an alternative choice, producing a newspaper clipping that announced a free lecture that evening. The world famous "demonologists" Ed and Lorraine Warren were on campus to lecture about their exploits. Paul looked at the two of them and said, "Chris, are you *kidding* me? You're going to go on a date with Jeff to see some ghost people instead of going out with these girls?" Chris, who wasn't in the mood for carousing, felt that he should accompany Jeff to the lecture as he was going to be alone; besides ... Paul was already planning to go out dancing with the girls anyway. To placate him, Chris mentioned to Paul that he would try to catch up with them after the lecture.

After Paul left, Chris told Jeff that he wasn't really sure that he felt like going to a lecture, especially one about ghosts. It seemed like a waste of time to Chris, time that could be better spent by reading about things like Bill Rodgers' record-setting 1979 Boston Marathon victory. "This stuff just isn't my thing. Maybe I'll just go back to the dorm," he said, but Jeff insisted: "Come on, it's only an hour long, and you don't really have to pay attention if it bothers you. I'd really just like someone to go with." Finally, Chris acquiesced and off they walked towards the building where the lecture would take place. After all, that is what friends do for one another.

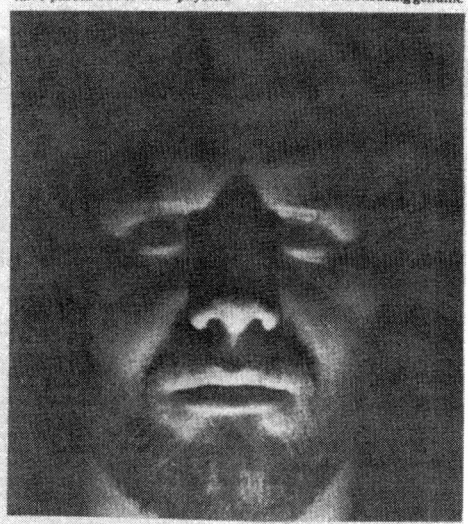

6. THE WARRENS

As the two walked towards the lecture hall, they were amazed to see students already lined up outside. Chris wondered what was so impressive about these two people who were going to speak that evening. He was unfamiliar with the name "Warren" and thought that it may have had something to do with a town near Herkimer, N.Y. that he had once read about. In reality, Ed and Lorraine Warren were known for being two of the first non-members of the clergy that researched and worked within the fields of Demonology, Possession and Violent Hauntings. Their exploits were well known, having been the subject of TV documentaries, as well as being a staple for every supermarket tabloid known to man.

The Warren's had a unique profession: the husband and wife team would go and investigate locations where people claimed to see ghosts. To them, it wasn't simply a hobby -- it was a major passion in their lives. Ed, a former police officer, and Lorraine, a self-professed "spirit medium," had formed the New England Society for Psychic Research in 1952. Having penned many books on the unusual and macabre, they claimed to have investigated well over ten-thousand paranormal cases during the course of their career. They are best remembered for their investigations of the Defeo murder site -- better known as "The Amityville Horror" -- as well as "The Demon Murder Trial" where the defendant claimed to have been possessed by a dark entity at the time that he murdered his landlord.

Ed and Lorraine were Roman Catholics who sincerely believed that most of the severest cases that they had investigated were the work of demonic entities. This belief often drew criticism from both those within and outside of the Church. Regardless of their belief system, the methodology used, or the controversy that surrounded their work, the two always drew a crowd wherever they lectured.

Chris sat in the darkened auditorium watching people with a skeptical eye. His assumption was that what the Warrens were going to talk about was just some hyped up sideshow banter. The reaction from the crowd was shocking to him -- they were absolutely enthralled by the presentation.

It was at this moment that Chris decided that if all these people were so interested in what the Warrens had to say, then he, too, should probably pay attention to them.

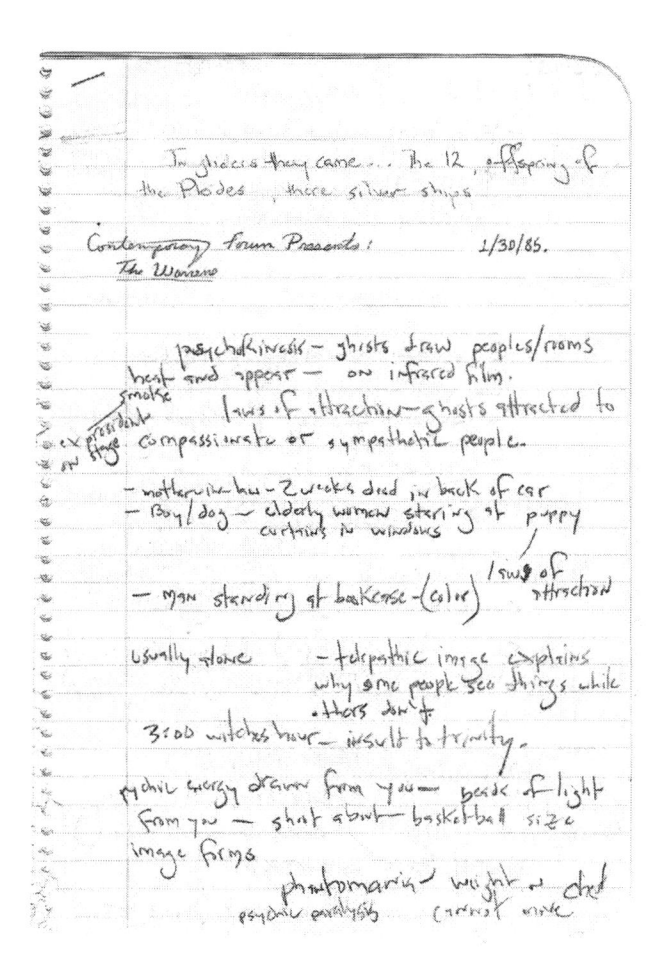

Above – Hand-written notes taken by Ungar and Di Cesare during lecture.

Ed and Lorraine described in detail many of the numerous experiences that they had encountered. They spoke of Ladies in White, Demonic Possessions, and a Raggedy Ann doll that had been treated as a living child by its owner. Somehow, it had become possessed by a spirit and would reappear even though the owner would lock it away. They also played alleged "spirit voices" that had been captured on their cassette tape recorders (now commonly referred to as Electronic Voice Phenomena or EVPs).

All of these stories served to unnerve Chris as they were outside the scope of his upbringing. He was shocked to realize that the more he listened to the recordings they played, the easier it got to make out what was being said on tape, and it unnerved him. He wanted to get up and leave several times, but each time Jeff calmly encouraged him to stay put.

At the end of the lecture the students were allowed to approach the Warrens in order to ask questions, get their autographs, and shake their hands. Many wished to accompany them on their upcoming ghost adventures, but the sum of $5,000 that was charged to cover an individual's expenses while on tour was a bit steep, especially when Chris realized that he had roughly $8 in his pocket; so traveling with the Warrens was out of the question.

When Chris approached the podium, a curious thing happened. Lorraine, who claimed to be a spirit medium, looked at Chris with obvious consternation. As he got closer and was extending his hand to shake hers, Mrs. Warren chillingly said, "I do not want to know my future." She glared at him with a gaze that was both wary and somewhat fearful. Upon hearing his wife's comment, Ed quickly stood up and stepped between them as if shielding his wife from Chris.

Seeing this reaction, Chris was both shocked and mortified. He felt very confused and disrespected by the way in which Mrs. Warren had reacted to him. Chris dejectedly shrugged his shoulders and walked away towards the exits. Jeff, in his typical manner, had jotted down several pages of questions that he had wished to ask the Warrens about the paranormal, but he made the decision to follow Chris up the aisle after he had turned and walked away.

It had been announced that, following the lecture, the Warrens would be visiting some of the dorms on the Geneseo campus looking for paranormal activity. Blake and Steuben Halls were rumored to be hotbeds of paranormal activity with strange mists, unexplained noises, and of course, the prerequisite white billowy figures seen wandering the halls. Even Monroe Hall had what was supposedly the ghost of a boy who, it was said, had somehow died during its construction. Students there claimed to have spotted him several times. Jeff asked Chris if he would like to go, but upset by Lorraine's perceived slight, Chris just said, "Jeff, those people obviously don't like me. You saw how they were rude to me. Why should I bother? No. That's it, I'm out of here." Observing how upset Chris was, Jeff decided to forsake the ghost hunt and hang out with his friend instead.

Chris did not say much as he and Jeff slowly made their way back to their dorm. Having been raised by his family to be polite to everyone, he couldn't fathom why this famous person, whom he had never previously met, said what she did. Chris felt a bit like some forlorn and rejected creature far from its home, one that had not belonged at the lecture in the first place. Jeff asked Chris if he did anything like "make a face" or some strange sound to offend them in some way.

"I didn't do anything!" Chris kept repeating. "I was sitting there right next to you! You would have known right away if I did!"

"Perhaps she sensed something in you," was Jeff's only comment.

Back in the dorm, Jeff began to pepper Chris with all sorts of questions about his childhood, his life back home and his ancestors in an attempt to discover if there was any type of genetic or environmental link that could have caused him to be in some way "sensitive enough" for Mrs. Warren to pick up on it.

In spite of the fact that he was still smarting from Lorraine's curt admonishment, Chris recalled that his great-great grandmother,

Maria Antoniette Ricciuti Fracasse, had been a fortune teller and that his great grandmother, Elvira Fracasse Barrar, had been a snake charmer in a traveling carnival show as a young woman.

Above – Di Cesare's paternal great-grandmother holding a python.

Could this have been what Mrs. Warren had picked up on?

That seems ridiculous, Chris thought to himself. Yet her words were still echoing in his head which gave him an unusual feeling of uncertainty.

It was on the night of the Warren's lecture that Chris first spoke about the world of the paranormal with anyone. Could this incident have been the harbinger of future events? Was it possible that Lorraine Warren may have felt or seen something had been long hidden and was now starting to build inside of Chris? Whatever the reason for her strange outburst, one thing was certain: from that evening on … life for Christopher Vito Di Cesare would never be the same.

7. I HEARD SOMEONE CALL MY NAME

It was Tuesday, February 8th, and the winter season in the Finger Lakes Region had become quite bitter. The winds that blow through the valleys bring with them pounding snow storms and sub-zero weather. For the students of Geneseo State it was especially cold. Chris found that even breathing outside became an exercise in pain. The slightest gust would cause the billowy snowflakes to swirl and almost obscure the walkway as he trudged back to his dorm. Stopping on the first floor to check his mailbox, he happily discovered a note telling him that a package was waiting for him in the office. Upon retrieving the box, he saw that it was a "care package" from home that had been lovingly assembled by his mother. Looking over the outside of the package he noticed a handwritten message that read: "Do Not Open Until Valentine's Day." This unexpected treat immediately brightened his mood and the chill of the outside world became something that could be tolerated.

During the winter months, some of the students of Geneseo State passed the days immersing themselves in their studies or enjoying whatever social activities the school and nearby town could offer. Others preferred to enjoy the company of friends, pooling their larders of snacks together and occupying themselves with games. One such favorite was the role playing game *Dungeons and Dragons*™. Every few weeks, Chris, Jeff, and other "would-be heroic characters" gathered round a pretend world and fight not only each other, but also monsters of all shapes and sizes. On one particular night, they had assembled in Chris and Paul's room to play. Chris was serving as Dungeon Master whose duty it was to be both the storyteller -- creator of the quest's make-believe world -- and the game's referee.

When at one point Chris began describing a horrible monster in great detail, Jeff told him to "stop it." Chris paid no attention to this, as would any other self-respecting Dungeon Master, and began to expound even more on its hideous depiction. Suddenly, the stereo, which was turned off at the time, produced a loud and ear pounding "POP."

Everyone jumped up from where they had been sitting. Jeff turned to Chris, and scolded him: "I told you to stop. No one ever listens to me. I told you not to do that!" He then walked out of the room. Without Jeff, the game ended and everyone took their half-eaten snacks and went back to their dorm suites.

All in all, Chris began to assimilate well into the fabric of college life. Not only was he doing great in his athletic pursuits but scholastically as well. For one of his classes he was required to do a lengthy oral presentation. Chris, who had always felt uncomfortable speaking before a crowd, had prepared for the talk and felt satisfied that he had performed well after it was over. A fellow student who had witnessed his speech walked up to him after class to congratulate him. As they were talking, Chris noticed something strange. The student -- bearded and bespectacled much like Jeff -- was looking at him with squinted eyes and had fixed his gaze a few inches above Chris' head. Before Chris could ask what he was staring at, his classmate replied, "Now I understand how you did so well. Everyone was mesmerized by you. You have an amazingly golden aura." Not knowing how to respond to this bizarre comment, Chris politely said "thank you" and quickly went on his way. In truth, he didn't even know what an aura was.

Auras are often described as a field of subtle, luminous energy or radiation surrounding people, animals or objects. Examples of aura's -- or what some religions call "aureoles" -- can be found in artistic renderings and are portrayed in the forms of halos that surround the heads of saints and deities. Chris told Jeff about this encounter, and later they would find on one of the college library's shelves a book on occult practices that contained an exercise that claimed to teach people how to actually see auras. Chris, Beth, Jeff and Craig, a former roommate of Jeff's, experimented on each other. They would alternate between attempting to see an aura and being the guinea pig that stood in front of a dark colored wall being stared at by the others.

Comparing notes afterwards, Jeff said that he saw nothing out of the ordinary. Craig and Beth, however, both claimed to see a golden or yellow haze surrounding both Chris' head and body. Not taking the experiment too seriously, it soon became viewed as just another meaningless diversion that had helped them stay busy in the hours between classes. Although Chris did take the time to record his aura.

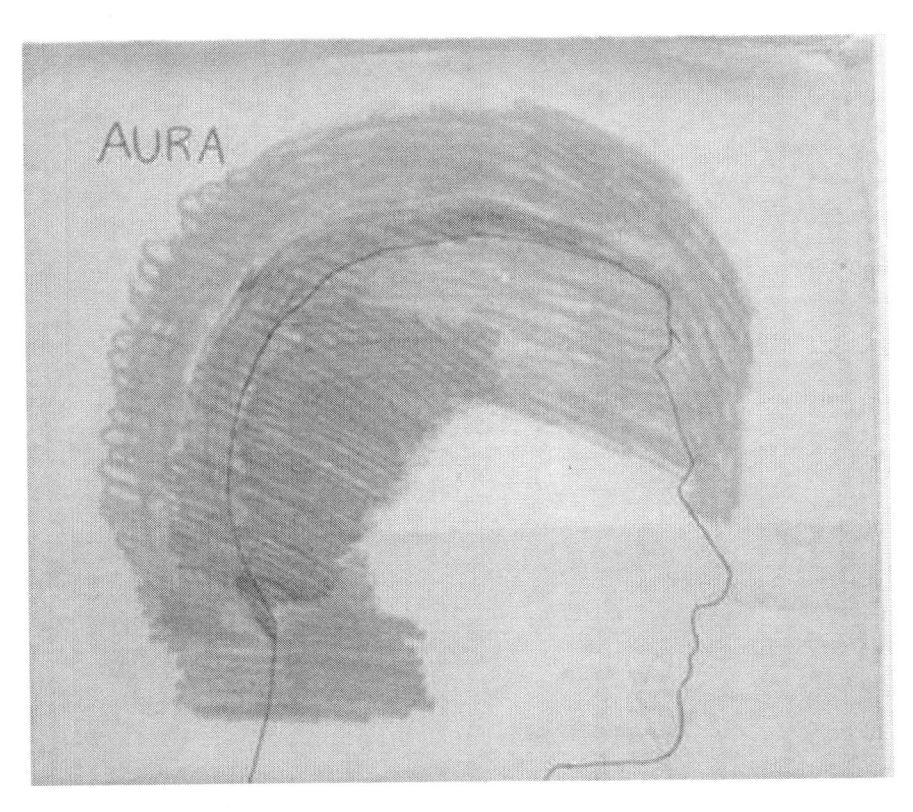

Above – Sketch by Di Cesare, while attempting to see auras with his friends.

Throughout the winter months, Chris continued his intense training routines all the while maintaining a sharp focus upon his studies as well.

During the first week of February, while he was reading in C2D1, Chris experienced a strong and unexpected shiver that ran throughout his entire body. He found this to be very unusual. Being a hardcore athlete, he regulated everything from his caloric intake to most of the factors of the environment in which he lived. This allowed him to look at life in an exceptionally analytical way. *For every action there is an equal and opposite reaction,* he faithfully recalled from his high school science classes. There had to be an explanation as to why he felt the unusually cold breeze flow through him. He just hadn't discovered it yet.

A few hours later, after he had completed his morning run, Chris was relaxing on the couch when he heard a slight creak emanate from the loft above. It was strange to hear the sound because this piece of furniture was well constructed with pieces of kiln-dried wood that were securely bolted together. Chris had not heard the sound before, even when several people had been moving around on top of the loft. He listened for a while, and when there was no further noise, he settled back into his running magazine. Again he heard a creak ... but this time, it was loud!

Geez, what the heck is going on? Is it an earthquake? he wondered. Looking around the room he noticed that nothing else was shaking. Searching for the most likely explanation, he reasoned that it must be Paul, who, because of his late nights, was probably still in bed. There had been several occasions when Chris had come back from a run and entered the dorm room never noticing that Paul was still asleep on the loft above him. Also, he reasoned, the loft supports might need to be tightened a bit. Chris yelled out: "Come on, Paul ...wake up! You need to get to class!"

Once, when visiting Paul's house, his parents had said to Chris, "We know that you're not his parent, but we live some distance away and can't always be there. College is very expensive -- can you do us a favor and once in a while get him moving and out the door for his classes?" Chris had agreed to help. It was the right thing to do.

Not hearing anything, Chris again yelled: "Come on Paul! You're going to miss your classes!" and the loft loudly creaked again. *Well, I'll fix his wagon,* Chris thought. He moved silently and swiftly out of the bedroom and retrieved a glass of cold water from the bathroom sink. He then began his climb up the ladder making sure that he did so carefully in order to keep the element of surprise in his favor. Lifting a foot from the first rung to the second, Chris was crouched and ready to pounce. Springing up while still holding the glass of water, he saw to his surprise that Paul's bed was empty -- there was no one in the room with him.

Now that's really odd, he thought, *My mind must be playing tricks on me. Why?* Climbing back down the ladder he decided that the only way for him to shake off the effects of this as yet unexplained incident was to focus on a task.

Chris needed to work on a paper for a class entitled "Ethno-Cultural Non Verbal Communication," which was due in a day or two. Not being entirely familiar with the subject, he assembled his notes and sat down at his desk in front of the typewriter. While he was pecking away at the keys, Chris heard a whispered voice call his name.

"What?" he asked. Only silence met his ears. *Come on already. I need to get this paper done. Stop fooling around,* he thought to himself. He checked in the hallway to see who had called him, but no one was there. After making sure that both his door and window were closed and locked, he settled back down to work.

Again he heard, "Chrisssss." This time, the sound of the "S" was more drawn out, as if whoever was calling his name was deliberately attempting to scare him. He quickly rechecked the loft and the result was the same; he was there all by himself. Having borne the brunt of several practical jokes at the hands of a senior classman the year prior, Chris reasoned that someone must be doing it again. Using logic, he felt that if he could somehow block out the sound of the prankster's voice that the joke would actually be on them; then they would be forced to cheerfully admit to doing it, and he could return to working in his paper.

Looking around the room, Chis noticed Paul's stereo headphones.

There's the answer to my problem, he reasoned. Turning on the stereo and placing the headphone unit on his head he found one of Paul's CDs and began playing Sammy Hagar's metal tune "I Can't Drive 55." Cranking it as loud as he could possibly stand it, he once again returned to his typewriter.

A few minutes passed and, to his satisfaction, no sound other than Hagar's head-banging beat was heard. Suddenly, over the blaring music, he again heard, "CHRISSSSSSSSS!" Impossibly hearing his name called again, Chris tore the headphones from his head and threw them onto the floor. Uncontrollably he began to shake as he thought, *Oh, my God, if this is a practical joke, this is the best one that I've ever heard of!*

Still reeling from what had just happened, he shouted across the empty room, "OK, guys, know what?! This is not funny. Cut the crap. I'm not laughing; I'm leaving."

Strongly irritated, Chris left the dorm to go out and get something to eat and then headed to track practice. All the while, as he walked across the sprawling campus, he kept waiting for someone to run up and say: "Gotcha! Oh man, dude, you should have seen the look on your face!" It never came.

After practice, still nervous, Chris returned to his dorm. But he heard nothing except the sounds of the quad's busy common area as he entered. That week, Chris, having been told that some of the gym's pipes had frozen, was forced to take a shower in his suite's bathroom instead.

While getting ready to undress, Chris suddenly felt a strong and unmistakable tug on his right leg. *What the heck?* he thought as the sound of his sweat suit's ankle snaps being pulled apart by unseen hands filled his ears. Chris yelled, "Oh, my God!" as he ripped the clothing from his body, grabbed his towel and bolted across the narrow hall into the quad's bathroom.

He leaped into the shower stall and slammed the shower curtain shut as if it would magically become a shield that could protect him from whatever he had just experienced. Chris stood there in silence for quite some time, his thoughts muddled and his body shaking from the cold air that swirled around him. His fear wasn't founded so much on the voice that had called his name, because he still felt that someone was playing a joke on him; rather, it was the recollection of being violated by unseen hands when something had pulled at his sweat pant leg that he found to be wholly unbearable. The mere thought of it made Chris nauseated and dizzy.

He peered nervously around the shower curtain from time-to-time, not knowing what -- if anything -- he might see. He 'knew' that he was alone but still could not shake the feeling that he was being watched. Yet, that feeling of being watched shouldn't have bothered Chris, and he knew it. He had run races in front of tens of thousands of cheering onlookers, some of whom were cheering specifically for him; and he had showered countless times in both high school and college locker rooms, around his teammates and athletes of all shapes and sizes. This feeling was different. This feeling made no sense. This felt 'wrong.'

Whatever was there -- in that room -- had begun studying him for some unknown purpose. Chris intrinsically sensed that this "thing" viewed him with some great feeling of envy. Perhaps as though an aging and injured man, confined to a wheelchair, might look upon someone whose legs were whole and whose future had few obvious limitations. In Chris' mind, whatever was out there seemed to *hate* him for being healthy, and alive.

Above – Photographs of the C2D bathroom, directly across from room C2D1 inside Erie Hall.

After a few minutes, Chris' initial "feeling" began to subside. He no longer sensed that the invisible presence was in the same room with him. Though calmer, he was still thinking twice about taking a shower. He had been standing in that shower stall for a good twenty minutes, but he did not want to turn on the water for fear that the noise of it would prevent him from hearing someone or something sneaking up on him. Visions of the Alfred Hitchcock movie *Psycho* filled his mind. All he could picture was Janet Leigh's character being stabbed to death in the shower at the Bates Motel. Chris decided he wouldn't leave the shower stall while there was no one in the suite, and he definitely needed someone to guard the bathroom door if he was to ever wash up.

Luckily, Paul happened to be coming back from class. He opened the C2D suite door and walked down the hall. Chris immediately knew it was him from the way that he whistled as he walked. He heard Paul put his key into the lock on their shared room's door, slowly opening it, a thud as he dropped whatever he had been carrying onto his desk. Chris now had a plan. Now that Paul was in their room, he could summon Paul into the bathroom by saying that he had to talk to him about something important. This being done, he could talk to Paul while safely showering.

Unexpectedly, Paul began screaming, "Oh shit!" and bolted across the hallway into the bathroom, closing the door behind him. He was so panicked he didn't realize that Chris was cowering in the shower himself. After a few seconds, Chris called out Paul's name, at the sound of which Paul freaked out screaming, "What's the matter with you? Why are trying to scare the crap out of me?"

Chris, trying to be cool, calmly said that he was in there because he was about to take a shower. Then using the plan that he had hatched while still hiding behind the shower curtain, he said, "I'll tell you what ... I'll take my shower and you can calm down. When I'm done, we can both go back to the room and talk about whatever happened." Relieved, Chris reached for the shower knob and turned on the water.

Eventually, the two left their bathroom safe zone and went back into their suite. Chris asked Paul to tell him about what he had experienced. Paul excitedly replied, "You aren't going to believe this -- I know that this is some crazy shit -- but ... " Chris wanted to know *exactly* what happened.

Paul explained that he had entered their room and placed his keys, wallet and books on his desk. Then he heard a distant sounding voice trying to talk to him.

"What was so unnerving was that it was calling your name. I'm telling you there was no one else, nothing in that room, and the voice was right by my head! It called your name twice!"

"That's pretty weird," said Chris, trying to not let on that he had experienced something very similar.

Originally, Chris thought that what he had experienced was some sort of prank. But now that Paul had also heard the same thing, he wasn't so sure. Perhaps he could find a logical answer if he could systematically sort out friends and acquaintances that might have the finances to pull off such an elaborate scheme; but that theory fell short in record time. Who would drill holes in their walls and place miniature speakers to broadcast the whispers that both had heard? Who possessed the electronic know-how needed to pull off such an elaborate practical joke? Chris asked himself, *Why us? What did we ever do to anyone to have someone do this?* Playing every possible scenario over and over in his head, nothing seemed logical.

The roommates decided to calm down by going to grab something to eat on campus at the Letchworth Dining Hall. At the end of the day, nothing calmed jittered nerves like some good, old-fashioned, cafeteria-style institutional food. Paul was still visibly shaken and they sat in complete silence while they ate. This silence was totally out of character for either one. Once again, Chris hoped that someone would walk over to their table -- a group of friends in tow -- and tell them how they were such losers after becoming so afraid of the prank played on them. He prayed that someone he or Paul knew would finally admit to being a part of this joke gone wrong. No one did.

Above – Additional notes by J. Jeff Ungar from the Warren's presentation.

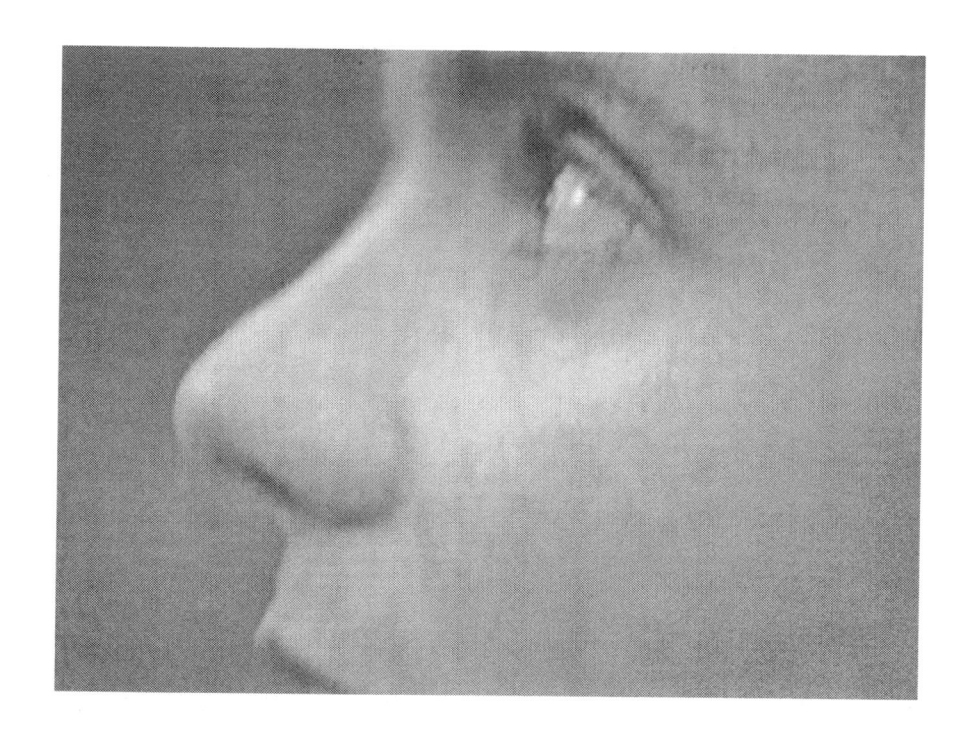

8. IT'S LOOKING AT ME

Returning to C2D1, they decided to try to calm down by concentrating on their classwork. Chris was sitting behind his desk, which faced the room's only door, reading a book when Paul let off a yell and said, "Stop it! You're pissing me off."

Chris had no idea what was going on and he was unsure whether he was in some way annoying Paul. Chris began to be conscious of any actions that he may have been doing, such as tapping a pencil, that might in be bothering his roommate.

A few minutes later, Paul said, "Cut the shit! I don't want to play these games."

Putting his book down, Chris focused intently on Paul and he watched as he swung his arms as if there were a bee buzzing around his head. He was making all sorts of erratic motions and angrily yelling: "Stop, I told you to stop!"

Chris called out to him and Paul's response, assuming Chris had been standing next to him the whole time, was: "How did you get back to your chair so fast?"

"I've been sitting here reading, Paul. I haven't left my chair," said Chris.

"Well you keep on blocking my light!" said Paul, sounding quite agitated. "The shadows that you keep making are going across my desk, they block my light and I can't see!"

"Dude, that is impossible," said Chris. "How can I possibly do that? I'm not Mr. Fantastic, you know. That would be cool, but it can't happen. There is no way!"

At this point, the visibly mad Paul jumped up out of his chair saying, "That's it! This place is getting fucking crazy!" and promptly left the room for several hours.

Closing and locking the door behind him, Chris sat down and took a few deep breaths before he began to calm down and mentally digest all that had just occurred. Whatever was happening was not just affecting him but now also his roommate.

Thoughts raced through Chris' mind: *The stuff that is now going on is something more than just a practical joke. What could be causing all of this? Are we part of some experiment where some unknown agent is adding drugs to our food? Could we have become the victims of some sort of gas leak or something that was perhaps sprayed into the room? Could we have been hypnotized and instructed not to remember the experience?'*

Anything that Chris could logically think of was reviewed in the attempt to solve the mystery of the voices and shadows.

Unfortunately, he could not come up with an explanation for any of it.

Seeking a break from the puzzle he was wrestling with, Chris remembered the Valentine's Day care package that he had received from his parents. Opening it, he found comfort in what he saw. There was a hand-knit sweater, some greeting cards, and at the very bottom of the box were some of his favorite candies: Hot Tamales®, the cinnamon flavored chewy treat that reminded him of more peaceful days.

Stuffing a handful into his mouth, Chris chewed gleefully until he began to feel overwhelmed by the strongest, most unfamiliar and most frightening feeling he had ever experienced. It was as if someone was standing directly behind him, staring; and this person's gaze was passing directly through his body.

This is impossible, Chris thought, *It's wintertime. The doors and windows are locked, and we are on the second floor to boot!*

Looking near the area that he felt the horrifying gaze was coming from, he caught in his peripheral vision what appeared to be a human form.

Chris froze where he sat. *Oh, my God, this is bad!*

His logical runner's brain took hold. *OK, Chris, let's get back to basics: What do you need to do to overcome this problem? You can punch your pillow; or better yet, you can count to ten, and when you get to ten, you can turn and nothing will be there!*

Counting slowly, still with a mouth full of candy, he began to count out loud, "One … two … " Reaching "seven," Chris stopped.

Above – The area of room C2D1 where the ghost first appeared, including Paul's stereo system.

Still in his peripheral view something was slightly behind him on the right-hand side. It still looked like a human form. Chris again tried to logically explain his way out of the situation. Was it merely the furniture that had been placed at just the right angle to produce what he was seeing? There was nothing like a large dresser or coat rack there that could produce this illusion. After exhausting every possible explanation that he could feverishly come up with, Chris slowly turned around and saw something that he had always clearly thought to be impossible: it was then that he saw -- for lack of a better term -- a *ghost*.

All the lessons taught to him by his parents and teachers could not prepare Chris for the sight he now witnessed. He had always been told that if someone claimed to have seen a ghost they were seeking attention, on drugs or mentally unbalanced. "Never fall for any of that stuff!" he was told.

Shock set in as Chris looked at what seemed to be an apparition floating before him, and Chris could make out its physical characteristics. It looked like a young man, perhaps late teens or early twenties, white complexion, brown hair, wearing an odd looking bluish coat or heavy shirt, with what may have been some sort of short, dark, leather-like pants. The entity's head was tilted unnaturally with eyes that stared blankly at him. Clearly tortured in appearance, the form's mouth hung open as if the jaw had been broken. Perhaps even more amazingly, Chris looked down and saw that its legs passed right into the stereo as if not solid! Right then, Chris realized that what he was seeing was something that could not be explained away with logic.

Mustering what little courage he had in reserve, he threw the box of candy into the air, screamed -- his eyes watering -- and bolted for the door. For the first time in his life, Chris found that not only could he not control his environment, he couldn't understand any of it as well.

Reaching the suite's hallway, Chris ran to the first door that he saw and began pounding on it. It was C2D2, the dorm room of Jeff Ungar and his roommate Ed. Hearing, "Help! I'm in trouble! Please, I need your help. Please!" Ed, who was alone at the time, became understandably wary, not knowing what to do. Jeff, who was watching a movie in another of the quad's suites heard the yells and looked down into the C2D hallway. Immediately, he ran over to see what had happened.

Seeing that Chris was in a state of shock, Jeff ushered him into his room and quickly began asking questions about what had just happened. Recounting the event, Chris begged Jeff not to tell Paul. Chris also asked him to begin writing things down in case he were actually losing his mind. This way, if it were true, doctors could read the journal and prescribe an appropriate treatment. In any event, Jeff, who was an English major, might be able to use the notes as the basis for a novel or something, Chris reasoned.

After telling both Jeff and Ed what he had seen, Ed immediately asked Jeff to get Chris out of their room.

Ed was greatly upset. "We don't need this stuff in our room," he said, "get him out now!"

Jeff looked at Ed directly in the eyes and said, "No, Ed, I just can't do that. He's my friend. He needs my help."

Chris then sat on the floor and began to breathe deeply in order to calm himself down. He explained to Jeff -- over and over again -- that he had panicked, but he wasn't saying why. After a few minutes, Jeff was finally able to discern the cause of Chris' panicked state: Chris was claiming that he had just seen a ghost in C2D1.

His eyes widening, but betraying no outward emotion, Jeff decided that he personally wanted to verify that something was happening in the room next door.

Chris piped up, "Jeff, I am telling you -- something strange is going on over there. This is no joke!"

At that, in typical Jeff Ungar style, he put on his vest, grabbed his notebook, pencil, a thermometer, his camera and whatever else he thought might be needed in order to validate -- or discount -- the strange story that Chris had just reluctantly shared. Once assembled, off he went to face whatever was in the room next door.

Chris wondered how Jeff could just calmly wander off and explore a room where something so traumatic for him had just taken place. To someone fresh from an unexplainable experience, it was inconceivable that anyone would step deliberately into a lion's den just to see if the lions were indeed hungry. Jeff would later explain that as a boy, he greatly enjoyed the television show *In Search Of* which was narrated by Leonard Nimoy. It was his eventual goal to experience something beyond the norm: to see a ghost, to experience meeting a vampire, to chase a Bigfoot, to observe an Unidentified Flying Object. This was his chance to fulfill one of his childhood dreams. He wanted to know that there was something beyond the everyday world of the mundane.

Chris was still sitting on the floor listening for any sounds that might come from his bedroom next door. All was silent. After about ten minutes he grew concerned and said to Ed that he thought maybe he should check on Jeff. Ed was relieved and said, "OK, just go. Get out of here already!"

With his heart racing in his chest, Chris entered the narrow hallway and walked the few steps to his bedroom door. Slowly peering into the room, he saw Jeff taking photos of objects, checking the temperature, touching the window panes, and methodically moving objects around. Chris watched in fearful amazement as Jeff bravely scoured the room.

Chris asked Jeff if he was alright. Jeff replied that he was fine and that he wasn't seeing anything all that unusual in the room. "However," he added, "your lights and clocks are flashing, and I felt an unexplained cold breeze coming from somewhere."

Finding nothing further they retreated back to C2D2 where Jeff told Chris, "I don't see anything happening at the moment, but I can tell from your emotional state that something did. Just stay close for a little while and we'll sit and talk about it."

As it was getting late, Ed said to both Jeff and Chris, "Listen, I'm not getting a motel room. I pay for this room, and I want Chris out of it already. Nothing personal, but I have classes in the morning, and I just don't need this kind of emotional drama in my life."

Agreeing, Jeff felt that it was probably a good idea for Chris to return to his room. He reassured him that if anything happened again that he would be just a room away.

After leaving the safety of Jeff's room, Chris crouched in the hallway between the bedroom doors, not knowing what to do. He was too scared to go back into his room alone. After about forty minutes, Paul came strolling back into the suite and asked what Chris was doing out there?

"Er, I'm getting some fresh air," said Chris. At which Paul snapped back, "By the bathroom?" (The bathroom was located, directly across from the door to C2D1). Chris felt like a "real dork" as he reflected on what he now judged as his rather stupid statement.

Shaking his head at Chris, Paul entered the room, got ready for bed, turned the lights off, and climbed onto his loft. Chris finally gathered his courage and decided that if Paul could do it, so could he. He quickly jumped into the bathroom to brush his teeth, all the while looking into the shower stall and checking behind him. Next, he sprang with a single leap back into his bedroom and locked the door. Like a five year-old child, Chris jumped onto the loft from the top of the ladder and once to his bed, he covered his head with his blankets.

9. NOW I LAY ME DOWN TO SLEEP

It was just after midnight on Wednesday, February 13th, 1985. One of his sisters would be celebrating her 17th birthday later that day with the rest of his family, hundreds of miles away. Chris was praying with all his might that the night would pass peacefully.

At the moment, all was quiet, and he was finally drifting off to sleep -- when suddenly, as before, he heard someone call his name.

Not again, he thought to himself as he pulled more blankets over his head in a feeble attempt to block out whatever was going on around him.

"Paul, will you please turn on the light?" he asked.

Overhearing this in the next room, Jeff thought to himself, *I hope that whatever is over there does not come into this room.*

As Chris lay on his side he could somehow feel a set of eyes staring at him. Summoning the inner strength that he had used to win hard-fought races, he peeked through the opening of his cloth fortress and was horrified to see the face of the apparition looking straight back at him several feet away.

Grabbing the blankets, he pulled them closed as if they were some magical armor that could not be penetrated by the ghost. He had regressed, momentarily, back into a child's hopeful thought process. He hoped that what he could not see could not hurt him; once again he tried to fall asleep.

That strange feeling of being watched overtook Chris once again. Peering out from under the blankets that still covered his head he saw what he perceived to be a partially-transparent face only a few inches from his own.

"Paul, I said turn on that light now!" he cried out so loud that it again startled Jeff from his slumber in C2D2 next door.

Begrudgingly, Paul reached for the switch, and in the glow of the incandescent bulb, neither one saw anything there. Paul switched the light back off, made some snarky comments and then fell back asleep.

Chris, who now sat up, resigned himself to the fact that he would have to suffer through the darkened night and try to make the best of it. As he lay facing the wall, he was startled again. This time the nightmarish creature was now somehow standing between the wall of the room and the loft which were separated by a few inches. Deciding not to call out to Paul whom he knew was already frustrated by the night's events; Chris again covered his head with blankets.

Sleep at last overtook Chris, but he was woken up once again. This time, it was by Paul. Chris jumped up and looked at his clock. The time was 3:00 A.M. (This early morning hour has been referred to as the traditional 'witching hour.' In Demonic studies, negative entities become more active at this time as it is the direct opposite of the time that Christ is said to have died on the cross).

"Chris, wake up!" Paul said in a hushed yet excited voice.

Now what was going on, Chris wondered.

"Somebody is in the room," Paul whispered.

"What? ... How do you know?" asked Chris.

"I hear them moving things below us," Paul meekly replied.

Both now could hear the sounds of objects being shuffled and moved below the raised beds. Paul described it as if "a desk chair was being rattled and dragged across the floor."

Not knowing what to do in this situation, Paul suggested that Chris go down and try to find out the source of the noises.

"What? Why do *I* have to go and check it out?"

At that moment Paul uttered the classic horror movie answer, "It's on your side of the room!"

After having seen the entity for the first time that day, heard his name repeatedly called out and gone through so much emotional turmoil, Chris could not think of anything to say that would get him out of this duty.

Quickly, Chris formulated a plan in his head. He would ever-so-slowly creep to the open side of his loft area and then jump from it while simultaneously kicking out like he had seen Bruce Lee do in many of his Kung Fu movies. Hopefully, he would kick anyone who had broken into their room. "But," he cautioned Paul, "I might need your help. If I do, I'll call out your name. Make sure you get down there quick."

Having been brought up a devout Roman Catholic, Chris remembered that in times of need that he should pray to God for aid. Crouching at the end of his loft, he made the sign of the cross and then leapt off. Unfortunately, he forgot that the actual beds were about two feet from the ceiling. Chris hit his head and fell straight down like a rag doll tossed from a bridge. Landing hard on his elbow and biting his tongue on impact, he realized that it was "game over" and he would certainly fall prey to whoever was in the room with them.

Chris cried out, "Paul, Paul!" waiting for him to appear like some imaginary cavalry in a spaghetti western movie. The seconds felt like hours, but Paul did not come down from the loft. As Chris lay there, he thought, *I just took myself out of the game because of total incompetence -- now what am I going to do?*

Pretending to have been knocked out by the impact of the fall, Chris, through squinting eyes, attempted to see if anyone was in the room. Seeing no one, he stood up and took stock of his battle injuries. His tongue was beginning to swell and his head and elbow ached terribly.

"It's OK, Paul -- there isn't anyone here," he said.

But just as Chris finished that sentence, they both heard a noise. Looking in the direction from where he thought the noise had come, Chris realized that his desk chair had been pulled out. Being a creature of habit, he knew instinctively that he had left it neatly tucked into the desk. He also found his desk drawers had been opened and that most of his text books had been pushed about.

Slowly, Chris began returning the chair and the drawers to their proper positions when he heard a "hissing" sound. Looking around, he remembered that there was a cassette recorder on the floor by his desk. Perhaps there had been a power surge that had caused it to turn on. Chris turned off the recorder, and scooted back up the ladder and back under the safety of his blankets, Paul denying that Chris had called his name.

Just as he was again drifting off to sleep, a single clicking sound was heard, and both roommates again heard the sound of a hissing tape cassette.

This time it was Chris who told Paul to go down and unplug the tape recorder and put it in one of his desk drawers and be done with it.

"There's no way am I going down there," was Paul's nervous reply.

After some debate, Paul said, "Listen, it's your tape recorder. You must not have turned it off right last time. Go back down and fix it!"

Chris became livid. "OK! Fine." he snapped. "I'll go back down there, unplug it, wrap the damn cord around it and put it in the desk drawer. Then I'm coming right back up here and I'm gonna' kick your butt!"

And, down the ladder Chris went.

He secured the recorder and thought, *I'm really going to give it to Paul for making me do this. What a jerk.*

Poised to climb back up the ladder, he instinctively turned and saw floating in the exact spot where he had just been standing -- and now still just inches from his head, neck and shoulder -- the spectral form of the ghost.

Chris' mind raced wildly. He wondered how long this "thing" had been standing next to him; watching him; perhaps even trying to touch him.

Chris grabbed a hard-plastic hair brush off his dresser and hoped that in some way it would serve as a lethal weapon to fight off this intruder. Picking his mark, as he learned from playing youth baseball, Chris threw the brush as hard as he could. The brush flew towards the chest of the entity dead on and passed through its chest ricocheting off the far wall and radiator with loud bangs.

Chris screamed and began racing up the loft's ladder in sheer terror.

It seemed to Chris that the world had somehow entered a dimension that was in slow motion. Even his utterance of "Oh shit" was long and drawn out in his ears. It seemed like it took forty-five minutes to climb from the bottom of the ladder up to the top. His stomach turned and muscles tightened as he climbed each rung as fast as his body -- honed from years of athletics -- allowed. The thought of a cold, dead hand grabbing his bare feet, piercing his skin and pulling him back down was all-consuming. At some point, he found himself cringing underneath his blankets in a fetal position. He began to sweat profusely, as if he were lying inside a blast furnace. The only sound was Paul's voice now worriedly asking, "What's the matter?" To which Chris replied, "Nothing. Just leave me alone. Don't talk to me."

His head was still swirling from both shock and the collision with the ceiling, and Chris couldn't remember a time -- including his fastest mile race on the track -- when his heart beat so fast and hard. He worried that it would tear through his chest as he heard Paul's voice saying, "Chris, someone is looking at me."

Chris held his breath in order to hear well. "How do you know?" he asked quietly.

Paul, now himself quite afraid, whispered that he could see the head of someone looking at him from the foot of his loft.

"Well, what does it look like?" Chris asked, careful not to influence Paul's observation in any way.

"I really can't tell," he replied, "But the head is tilted sideways."

This was all that Chris needed to hear. Previously, he had not said anything to Paul about what he had seen. There, in that darkened room, Chris, who was always looking for an explanation for what was happening, suddenly knew it had not been a hallucination. It was real and now someone else had seen it. Chris thought to himself, *I don't really know what it is; but I know it's* dead, *and I am in big trouble!*

Throughout the rest of the night Chris heard the sounds of more unseen movement below. In times of peril he had been told to find peace in his religion. After what he had seen, Chris reached for a Bible that he had brought from home and squeezed it to his chest. He then remembered that there was another item that would bring him some peace. Sitting on the top of the couch below him was a pillow which had a picture of Jesus Christ on it. Ever so slowly, Chris reached his hand between his mattress and the dorm room's back wall. Feeling around in the darkness, he finally felt the pillow's smooth fabric and pulled it up.

Still unnerved by the whole experience, Chris knew that he might not be able to sleep that night. He decided to just try to lie still on his loft and let the night pass slowly by until he could find safety in the light of dawn. Even though he was still under blankets, he again felt that now too familiar chill passing over his body and the "knowing" that someone was once more staring at him. Looking into the dim light of his room, he spied in front of his closet door the ghost still glaring at him with those dull lifeless eyes and that crooked head.

In his overtired brain, logic was again attempting to explain what he was seeing. *Is what I am seeing just my eyes playing a trick on me? Could I be making myself insane seeing shadows at crazy angles?* he wondered. Reaching out, he placed his hand in front of what little light was shining into the room and saw that the shadows that he produced were not slanted in the same direction as where the ghost appeared.

Emotionally and physically exhausted from the evening's terrors, Chris finally fell into a short and fitful sleep. Paul, who had feigned to be asleep while all this was going on, peeked out through half-opened eyes and saw what he thought looked like a gold colored "ball of light" floating near Chris's head.

As the room gradually was illuminated by the rising sun, Chris awoke and decided to check out his belongings, to make sure that nothing had been "touched" by the ghost while he had slept. Taking a quick inventory, he found that his desk chair was once again moved, his alarm clock which had been set to ring at 8:10 A.M. was reset to 9:16 A.M., and a photo frame which contained the photo of his baby cousin had been taken apart. *Why is this happening? Why is it messing with my stuff?* he wondered nervously.

[9:16 on TRUTECH digital clock]

Still groggy, Chris thought it best to try to follow his normal routine. However, as he was getting dressed, he felt something gently hit his clothing as though being dropped on him from the ceiling above. He then noticed three drops of a slimy white substance on his pant leg just above his right knee.

Could this have been ectoplasm? During the last century, mediums were producing it at every séance they conducted. He had learned that from the Warren lecture.

"Screw all of this," he tiredly mumbled as removed the pants and threw them into the trash can. He then pulled on a long-sleeved button down shirt.

Unfortunately, each time that he would try to button one cuff, the other mysteriously unbuttoned.

"Damn it! You're not going to keep me from getting out of this room," Chris said, as he grabbed up some additional clothes and stormed into the bathroom to finish dressing.

That morning, before going off to class, Chris left Jeff a message on their suite's door: "Have I got a story for you!"

Incredulously, Paul at some point must have seen the note and scribbled out the message's contents. It was clear that he was beginning to find the ghostly visitation not so amusing.

When Chris finally met up with Jeff later that morning, he went over the highlights of what had happened the previous night with him. Amazingly, Paul clandestinely did the same. This would aid Jeff in his research as he never told one about the other's confession to him to avoid cross contamination of the witnesses' accounts. For an observer like Jeff, receiving two accounts of the same occurrence gave him a more complete picture of the actual situation. Jeff wanted to really help his friend get through whatever it was that was troubling him. He would analytically record in his ever growing journal everything that related to this haunting. It was his meticulous recording and lending of a sympathetic ear that helped Chris deal with all that he had been going through. As for the results of the spirit's nocturnal antics, Chris was able to salvage three hours of sleep and the residual stress caused him to fail an important psychology test.

10. WHAT TO DO?

The evening of February 13th offered another stretch of cold blustery winds sweeping through the valley, and Chris in his typical fashion was laboring to finish a paper that was due the next day.

The room had been decorated with red and white balloons in honor of St. Valentine's Day. Paul was busy studying at his desk when all of a sudden -- *POP! O*ne of the many balloons exploded. Both having been focused on their individual work jumped at the shock of hearing the sound. Catching their breath and smiling at their own frightened reactions, they went back to what they had been previously doing. Then *POP* went another balloon, then another and another ... *POP!*

"Stop that!" Paul yelled, "Something is breaking the balloons!"

POP, POP went two more.

"Why do you think it's happening?" Chris asked, almost in a daze. Checking the ones that were closest to his desk, he found nothing unusual about them.

POP went a balloon that was closest to the door. "See THAT?!" said Paul as he exited the room to find someone else to witness what was happening. A few moments later, he came back with one of their suitemates who did not really take the incident seriously. "I'm telling you, they all started popping literally at the same time by themselves!"

Becoming frustrated, Paul stomped out of the room followed by the suitemate, leaving Chris alone.

The next day, Chris noticed that the temperature in his room was colder than usual. Pulling on a sweatshirt he settled back into his routine of alternating his studying with reading a runner's magazine. This one was a recap of the 1984 Olympic Games.

Out of the corner of his eye, he saw that the drapes were moving as if a slight breeze was brushing by them. *Who would leave the window open in February?* he wondered. Paul could have opened it for some crazy reason and had just forgotten to close it. But after checking the window, Chris found that it was tightly shut. Even after running his hand around its metal frame, he could find no source for the breeze.

As his back was turned to the door, the cold and tingling sensation that he was being watched returned. The air seemed to have become heavier and his heart began to race. He spun quickly around only to discover ... that there was no one there. Chris breathed a sigh of relief.

Paul had started to call their ghostly visitor "Tommy." He didn't have a reason other than it just sounded right. "Tommy" by now was starting to become an annoying part of dorm life.

Jeff and Chris had spent much of the day in Jeff's room next door. Jeff -- who for all intents and purposes was totally fascinated by the notion that there was a ghost living in the suite with them -- wanted to conduct more experiments during his non-classroom time. Chris, temporarily enjoying the luxury of the light of day, was also taking things in a calmer fashion, agreed. In fact, he even began joking a bit about "Tommy" which seemed to be the only slightly effective way he found for dealing with the situation.

With Paul and Ed out of the dorms, the two friends reentered C2D1 around 5:00 P.M.. By now, Chris and everyone else had designated the couch located under his loft the "Negative Zone" because of all the strange breezes and sightings that had been occurring there. A chill was immediately noticed as they walked into the room and a slight breeze was detected near Chris' side of the loft. Slowly, the closet door began to open by itself.

Wanting to engage the spirit and test the limits of his newly discovered courage (which Jeff thought was not a good idea) Chris said, "Tommy, can you come out and play?"

There was no reply.

Looking around and seeing that the room was still all in order, Chris repeated the request. Gradually, a low, guttural sound began to audibly build in the room. It sounded as if it were coming from right next to Chris, as if attempting to say his name. Shocked by the response, Chris ran from where he was standing towards Jeff, who claimed to hear nothing. Looking around as he ran, Chris could see the blankets on his loft move, slightly rising into the air, and then an indentation as if someone were sitting on the loft's mattress became clearly visible. Just before slamming his door shut on his way out, Chris heard something that raised the hair on the back of his neck. Unmistakably, he heard a loud, prolonged sigh.

Following the example of his father, Chris was determined to rationalize what was going on. In this way he might be able to uncover some explanation as to why he and Paul both were experiencing this chilling phenomenon. The only problem was that nothing seemed to fit. The world that Chris had grown up in and which had given him security and safety throughout his life was teetering on the edge of a great dark abyss. Each time that he witnessed this errant spirit, he felt as if somehow all he knew was wrong. The possibility that he was going insane had crossed his mind a dozen times. This entire episode was forcing Chris to accept the fact that, in the scope of the universe, he did not actually possess a lot of knowledge ... or power. For someone who craved to be in control of his environment, this was a devastating concept. Finally, Chris began to accept the fact that these crazy events just might be paranormal in nature.

Chris began to have a difficult time sleeping. Every creak and groan the lofts made was amplified tenfold in his mind; every muffled voice from the quad's common area became a demonic whisper bringing with it absolute feelings of dread. Night after night, Chris jolted awake, ready to defend himself, whenever the suite's outer door would close or a toilet would flush.

Continuously, Chris would ask Paul to keep the room light on; and Paul, tired of Chris' pleading, would become angry. Paul needed the room to be dark in order to sleep, and since the loft was only a few feet from the ceiling, the light from the ceiling fixture would be blinding to him. They both wondered how much longer this would go on -- why were they being targeted and what could they do about it? Apparently, no one else was having a problem in the quad. But because of the nightly ruckus, some suitemates began to look at Paul and Chris in a much more cautious light.

Chris gave serious thought to changing rooms, but it was highly unlikely that he would be allowed to do so. In the first place, once it got out that his room was allegedly haunted no one would want to stay in there. Secondly, if Chris deceived someone into changing rooms and never said anything to the fellow student about a ghost, he would be a bad person, which went against everything Chris had been taught since childhood. Finally, he wasn't allowed to move. Chris had already gone to talk to the Resident Director and asked for another room. She said that regardless of the reason, they just could not move him, explaining that if they made an exception, then they would have to move anyone who wanted a change, and that would be a huge headache. She went on to say that if he still insisted on changing rooms, it would have to wait until after the semester ended.

With no options available, Chris knew that he would just have to steel himself against whatever was haunting C2D1.

While he was still quite wary of the situation and fearful of seeing "Tommy," his anger and frustration were beginning to boil over. Chris knew that something had to be done ... but what?

Jeff Ungar had a plan: they would try to photograph the ghost.

On Valentine's Day, with camera in hand, he calmly walked into Chris' room and began to snap away. He concentrated first on all of the corners of the room, and then expanded the shots to include Chris' desk, chair, closet and the lofts. For Jeff, it was important to photograph the room not only for the possibility of a ghost appearing, but also to establish a baseline for future examination in case someone else should ever have a problem in there. During the photo shoot, Jeff took most of the pictures; Ed from next door poked his head in and took two shots from the doorway; and it was Chris who took the last shot.

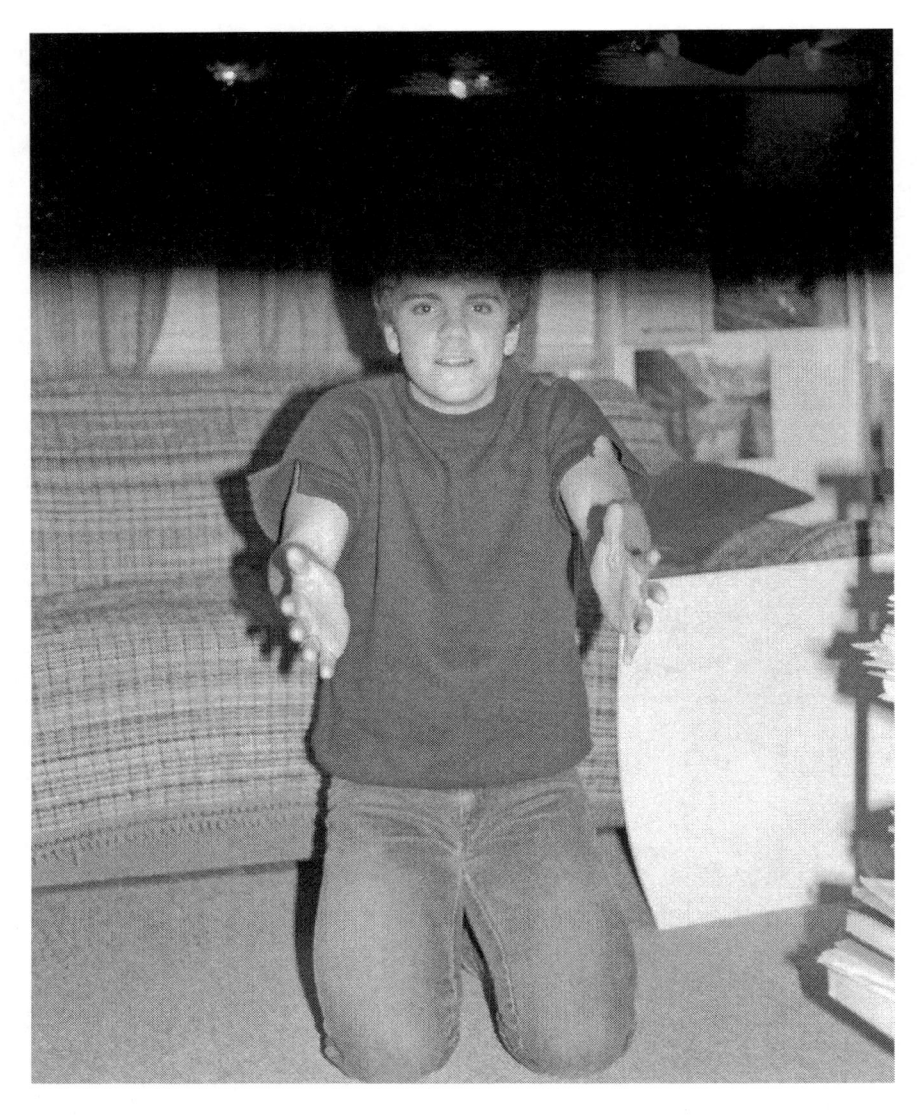

Above – One of the C2D1 Haunting's iconic photographs. Taken by J.Jeff Ungar, this image shows one of the effects of the ghost's presence: A strong, cold wind that forces back both of Di Cesare's sweatshirt sleeves and the large piece of cardboard construction paper behind him.

The next day, February 15th, Chris was disheartened to find out that Jeff was leaving on a seven-day Florida vacation with his family. Jeff had proved to be his rock during most of the insanity and Chris was worried that getting through the next week without him would be difficult ... and perhaps even dangerous. No one knew what was going to happen next.

That night, both Paul and Chris were again kept up all night being terrorized by "Tommy." The ghost was becoming bolder: the more it acted, the more it seemed to crave the reaction it would get from its intended 'victims.' It was almost as if "Tommy" was honing his skills and becoming stronger with each passing night.

When things would start to quiet down, Chris would catch sight of something black whisk by him. It almost seemed as if the ghost was moving just slow enough for them to notice the movement yet quick enough so as not to allow them to actually *see* what it was. Other times, Chris would turn and "Tommy" would be right there, *BOO!* just inches from his face.

To make matters worse, Chris would feel something icy cold touch his left ear, cheek and neck, which would then became cold and numb. Unable to take any more, Chris would scream in horror and run out into the hallway to compose himself. Each time they returned, the roommates would sit in silence awaiting the next assault by the spirit.

The night passed slowly, but Chris was finally able to fall into a light, fitful sleep. Paul, who was still awake, noticed some movement from the foot of his sleeping area. When he looked over in that direction, there stood "Tommy," head violently wrenched to one side as if it had been snapped with great force. Blank, dark eyes stared back at Paul. He froze in revulsion and horror. Closing his eyes he wished with all his might for the creature to go away.

Totally exhausted, he must have fallen asleep, because the next time he looked at the clock, several hours had passed. He woke Chris up and told him what he had seen. Together they sat up the rest of the night talking about what they should do.

Paul was miserable. He kept telling Chris about the possibility that maybe "Tommy" was planning to eventually torture and kill them both, and by some supernatural force, take their bodies to a place where they would never be found. Chris, by this time, was totally spooked and pleaded with Paul to be quiet. The roommates' emotional paranoia was reaching a fever pitch.

But Paul kept on repeating: "We have to do something or we are going to die!"

They knew that something had to be done immediately, or they would have to leave the campus. For Chris -- the second person in his family to ever attend college -- leaving was not an option. College for him was a matter of personal pride and family reputation.

11. A SINGLE CANDLE IN THE DARK

Both Paul and Chris were exhausted after suffering through yet another night of "Tommy's" antics. As the morning sun slowly rose over the snowy campus streets, the two dressed and set out on a mission that they had decided upon doing during their forced night vigil. They had agreed to bring in a professional, someone who had experience in these unearthly matters. It was Paul who had suggested that they seek out the help of clergy. So at 7:00

A.M., the two forlorn looking students trudged off through the fresh snow to St. Mary's Roman Catholic Church where Chris regularly attended Mass. Of all the places they had considered, Chris reasoned, the Catholic Church would not turn them down.

Pressing the rectory's doorbell, Chris was apprehensive about the kind of greeting that they would get. It was still early morning, but Chris knew that priests would drop everything to help someone truly in need -- at least that was what he had been taught in his Catechism class.

The door opened with a creak and there stood a matronly looking woman who identified herself as the rectory's housekeeper. She naturally asked them what was it that they wanted, and Chris gave her a greatly abridged version of what was going on. Looking as they did -- like they had just stepped out of an alien spacecraft -- she told them to wait and quickly closed the door. A few minutes later, she returned with a small bottle of holy water, a rosary and a piece of paper with the name of a local minister on it that she suggested they talk to.

"Good luck," she said and closed the door.

To say that Chris was disappointed by this treatment was an understatement. After all, these people were supposed to deal with this type of crisis, not pawn it off on someone else. Images of Christ driving out demons were shattered as the rectory door closed in his face.

Disillusioned, the two trudged through the powdery snow back to the campus. Too upset to immediately look at the name on the paper, Chris stuffed it in his pocket and thought that he would do something about it later.

The ghostly visitations of "Tommy" were now becoming a nightly occurrence. With each visit, it seemed as if the spirit was getting stronger, as if the spirit was craving their attention in much the same way that a drug addict craves his next fix. Like a parasite, it seemed to be growing 'fat' on the fearful emotions of the residents of C2D1. Chris, forever being a person who looked for control in his life, decided to try to learn how to better "sense" when "Tommy" would be near. He would attempt to remember how he felt and what was happening around him just before the ghost made its presence known. While this effort may not have been 100% successful, it did serve to empower Chris in the belief that he was doing all that he could to deal with the ongoing situation.

It seems quite fortunate that Chris was able to establish a wonderful group of loyal and caring friends that he could surround himself with. When a student is away from home, they often tend to feel isolated. That is until they can connect with like minds by which they can form bonds of friendship. One such person was Beth Kinsmen who Chris had met through his roommate Paul. Beth and Paul had dated very briefly, and Chris felt it best that they remain friends. As close as he and Beth had become, Chris knew that he could not begin a romance as long he was still focused upon his Olympic dreams.

On February 17th, Beth and Chris were cramming for tests in the common room of the C2D suite when something caught their eyes. It wasn't so much the object but the movement that the object made which unnerved them so. A pencil dropped from the ceiling, hitting the floor with a light clicking sound, then rolled towards them and stopped at their feet. Both sat in stunned silence for a few moments and Chris began to examine the ceiling from where they believed the pencil had fallen from. The ceiling was intact: no holes for anything to pass through were visible.

After telling Paul of this incident, the three sat down and tried to rationally decide what they should do next. Since moving from the room was out of the question, the next step was trying to figure out how to survive the rest of the semester.

Several options came up for consideration. Chris and Paul thought that perhaps they should begin spending more time away from C2D1, and perhaps even Erie Hall itself. They both agreed that at first glance it was a great idea, but that it would only be effective during the day. What about the nights? And where would they sleep?

Beth had done some research and found additional information on Dr. Lawrence Casler, her psychology professor. It seemed great news to her that he both taught on campus and had an interest in parapsychology. Maybe he would have some suggestions that would help their situation?

Above – Note from Beth to Chris with contact information For Dr. Casler.

Another avenue to consider was asking their parents if they could quit school and come home -- temporarily. Again, for Chris, this was not an option; but for Paul, it might prove to be a way out.

Lastly, they could track down the name that the housekeeper at St. Mary's had given them.

The evening of February 13th offered another stretch of cold blustery winds sweeping through the valley. Chris, in his typical fashion, was laboring to finish a paper that was due the next day.

12. THE BLEAK AND DREARY WINTER

"In the bleak mid-winter frosty wind made moan / Earth stood hard as iron, water like a stone / Snow had fallen, snow on snow, snow on snow / In the bleak mid-winter long ago." -- Christina G. Rossetti, 1872.

To Chris, the gray sunless days filled with cold temperatures were trial enough. Having to endure the increased paranormal activity in his room night after night was beginning to take its toll. His grades began to fall and even his passion for running had now become more of a chore and he missed practices regularly. "Tommy's" nightly visits now were beginning to affect Chris more than he cared to admit.

Paranormal activity is extremely hard to prove. Whenever such claims are brought to light they must first be examined for organic causes. It has been discovered that the time of year can act as a catalyst to produce many supernatural-like experiences. For example, the medical community has accepted that there is a condition that affects many people during the winter months. Its name is "Seasonal Affective Disorder" -- better known by its acronym: "SAD." Symptoms of this ailment include sleep problems, sadness, increased stress and anxiety, emotional outbursts such as crying, loss of desire to take part in activities (especially sports), and becoming withdrawn from social outlets. It is not unusual to see college students miss more classes or stay huddled in their dorm rooms during this time of year. When these symptoms occur, any person who is experiencing them should seek a medical evaluation. This will rule out a physical cause for the disturbances that they may claim.

A perfunctory assessment might initially allow that Chris could have been struggling with a severe winter bout of SAD. But he had already endured the previous winter with no ill effects, and the preponderance of conflicting evidence just doesn't support this notion. No, the situation in C2D1 was rapidly becoming far worse than anything the long New York State winters could throw at him. The phenomena experienced now by several occupants of the C2D quad bordered on being classified as a "Violent Haunting." This type of intense paranormal activity is considered more problematic than what is typically thought of as a 'noisy ghost' or poltergeist.

According to Raymond Buckland's *The Spirit Book*: "It is incorrect to speak of poltergeist energy as malevolent energy, because it is impersonal, and although usually emanating from an individual, is not directed by that individual, either consciously or unconsciously. It is pure energy running wild."

What Chris and Paul were now suffering through was something different than outbursts of random psychokinetic energy. Some type of intelligence seemed to be present and bent on terrorizing and wearing them down physically.

In rare cases, there can be something more sinister that may be taking place: it is referred to as "Infestation." During this type of haunting, activity begins slowly. It grows stronger with each encounter while becoming focused on one individual. The activity then begins to change into attacks on that particular person.

Other phenomena occurs such as nightmares; moving of items; the sounds of movement; the desecration or destruction of religious objects; raps and banging on walls, ceilings, and doors; cold spots; touching, pokes, and slaps; and an indescribable feelings of hopelessness.

Above – Looking into a 'quad' from a 'common area' in Erie Hall.

According to the tenets of Demonology, the purpose of such phenomena is intelligently designed to systematically wear an individual down to the breaking point.

Social isolation is sometimes the result of Infestation. It is a method where close personal relationships can become severed, depriving the individual of the objective opinions and observations of others. It will then open the door to the next phases of the attack which are "Oppression" and then possibly "Possession."

In overall terms, Infestation is considered the first phase of "Spirit Possession." Spirit Possession is a process by which a demon or human spirit will enter into the life of a human being, causing them to break mentally, physically and spiritually in order to gradually destroy their will. Its express purpose is the possession of that human's soul through the debasing of that individual until they enter into an animal-like state of being, or end their torment through death.

In most cases of possession, the individual in some way *invites* a negative entity into their lives.

Many who become afflicted by the beginning stages of possession or become targeted by an entity will seek help through various religious rites and rituals.

The most commonly used is the "Rite of Deliverance," which is used to cleanse a location of negative energies or influences. This is sometimes effective; however, in many cases, it will only serve to lessen the present activity. Other times -- especially in those cases classified as "Intelligent Hauntings" or Infestations -- the paranormal activity will actually amplify.

Unfortunately, there is a great deal of trial and error required in determining the cause, as each specific case is different.

Compounding this problem is that most clergy are not trained to assist and carry out these types of rituals.

Lastly, there are cases where spirits will attempt to contact and attach themselves to humans through what is theorized in some metaphysical circles as being part of the "Natural Laws." This is where two or more similar 'vibrations' are attracted to one another.

Many believe that there is an entire world of spirits, spirits who feel attached to a location because of emotional trauma. They do not move on to a 'higher plane' of existence, and thus are bound to that location, looking for some way to establish a form of communication whereby they maybe find some understanding and gain eventual release from their current condition.

These situations may also include not only those who are seeking out living individuals with whom they have similarities in personality, but in some rare cases, those who may have an actual ancestral link with a spirit.

In these cases, the spirit will 'act out' in order to gain the attention of the person they are attempting communication with. As with Infestation, it usually begins very slowly.

If notice is not being returned, the spirit will increase its level of activity until it gets what it longs for. This is normally considered to be an Intelligent Haunting.

Once begun, the only way to stop the progression is to take charge of the situation as soon as possible in order to regain absolute control before it escalates into something potentially violent.

Those individuals who have solid 'core beliefs' are more likely to find themselves targeted by negative entities; however, they do seem to fare much better than those who do not have a strong belief system.

Control in these spiritual matters is extremely important.

As for Chris and the other residents of C2D quad, would this realization come in time?

13. THE OPPRESSED

"Science had failed me, my education had failed me, my instincts had failed me, my running training had failed me. I had one thing left, which was my religion." -- Chris Di Cesare, Haunted Survivor.

Chris felt as though the proverbial rug had been pulled out from under him. There were so many things that he had once taken for granted that were now missing from his life.

Paul and Chris had made up their minds to seek out the priest that the housekeeper at St. Mary's had referred them to. Chris recalled that during their conversation at the rectory's door, she had said that Father Charlie Manning had shared a few ghost stories of his own.

They discovered that Father Charlie was actually ministering at the Interfaith Center on campus. As a staunch Roman Catholic, Chris had always gone to St. Mary's for his devotions and never felt the need to seek out another place of worship. In his mind, the concept of anything "Interfaith" seemed to be a watered down version of what he was used to practicing, but he reasoned that it might be his only hope.

In order to try to stay grounded during this confusing time, Chris attempted to surround himself with objects that held special meaning to him. And just like Linus, the thumb-sucking boy in the *Peanuts* comic-strip who had a blanket, Chris had what he called his "Jesus pillow" which his mother had made for him.

One night as he was trying to fall asleep with much difficulty, the entity once again began to hover near Chris' head. He could see its crooked neck and black eyes. The temperature in the room dropped so dramatically that it was like he was sleeping in a meat locker.

While Chris kept his Bible with him at all times -- even in bed -- he felt that he needed something more. Reaching down between the wall and the loft's mattress, he searched for the Jesus pillow which he had remembered was on the couch below. Worried that something might happen to him, he asked Paul to watch and make sure that he would be safe from anything that might try to grab his arm.

"If you are my friend, Paul, please watch," Chris implored.

Paul agreed that he would.

Feeling around for the fabric of the pillow, Chris snatched it up quickly and hugged it to himself.

Seeing that Chris was now sitting upright, Paul asked "You good now?"

"Yup, I am," said Chris, as he placed the Jesus pillow on top of the others.

But just as he laid his head down on it, the pillow was forcibly yanked out from under him.

"Put the light on!" he screamed.

Paul fumbled for the desk lamp's switch and just as he turned it on, he witnessed something that in his mind was virtually impossible: *Chris was engaged in a tug of war with an invisible opponent.*

He watched in amazement as Chris tried to move the pillow. At first it seemed to give a little but then suddenly would not budge, as if it were glued in place. Chris grabbed the pillow tighter and pulled as hard as he could which only resulted in it moving a short distance.

Breathing heavily, Chris was visibly shaking as both he and Paul witnessed the pillow suspended in *mid-air*. Despite the seeming impossibility of the pillow's position, Chris dug his feet into the sides of his mattress and tugged even harder.

"Let go of my damned pillow!" he screamed.

Paul was in total disbelief. "Oh my God, no one should ever have to see this!"

Struggling to regain ownership, Chris screamed at the entity one last time and pulled with all his strength. The pillow then finally broke free and fell to the mattress, while the force of his pull sent Chris slamming into the wall beside him.

This 'attack' shook Chris up more than anything that had previously transpired. It was as if whatever this thing was had now tried to take something that was both a comfort to Chris and represented a very important part of his faith.

These nocturnal attacks were taking a heavy toll.

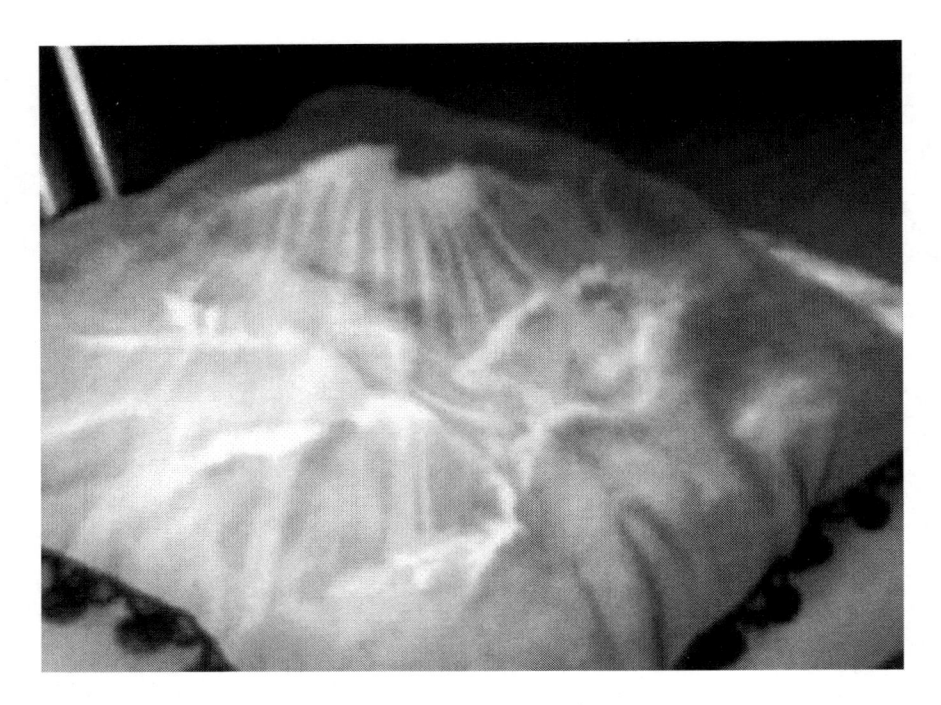

Above – Pillow that Paul watched Chris struggle for against an unseen adversary in room C2D1.

Chris, who had once thrived on running, now stopped attending the Winter Track practices. His worried coach called him to find out why. Not wanting to reveal the truth, Chris merely said that he just was not feeling up to par and that he would assuredly return for the upcoming Spring Track season.

Although Coach Kentner may have taken the answer at face value, Chris' inner circle knew better. With a falling grade point average and a lack of mental focus he might not still be on campus when the snows melted.

More alarming than his grades was the fact that the intensity of the paranormal activity was increasing almost daily. The ghost became even more brazen in its attempt to demand Chris' attention.

One evening, he was sitting shirtless at his desk and felt the icy cold pressure of an unseen hand upon his shoulder. Lunging from his chair, Chris fell onto the floor, again rolling up into a fetal position. Lying there, he prayed to God like he had never prayed before, "Please make my life *normal* again. Take this ghost away from me!"

Looking up, he saw a poster that was tacked to his dorm room wall. It was a poster from the science fiction film *2010: The Year We Make Contact*. Chris wondered if God was even going to allow him to live until 2010 with all that was going on.

Jeff Ungar had returned from his Florida vacation around the 25th of February. Chris and Paul quickly filled him in on what had happened. They all agreed that it would be a good idea to talk to the campus priest and the suggestion was made that Jeff could use the rest of the week to complete his notes. In this way they could present to Father Charlie a complete picture of what was occurring.

Chris felt that it was important to give the priest a comprehensive log of events rather than sitting there and blurting out a story that seemed crazy even to him. Jeff agreed to do this; however, he insisted that if they were going to take his journals to the priest for examination, that they make sure he got them back -- and all were in agreement on that point.

While Jeff busied himself with updating his notes, the phenomena continued to plague Chris. As the week dragged on, he felt as if he were on autopilot, merely attending classes and going through the motions without the previous passion for all he did. Others could see the changes in Chris. His body which had once been chiseled from the grueling workouts now became alarmingly thin. His once legendary appetite disappeared and he now only ate to comply with the worried appeals of his classmates.

The once happy-go-lucky student, who would go streaking down the hallways for a good laugh, had now become more sullen and serious than ever before. To those around him, it was as if someone had clicked a switch inside of Chris. To his friends and acquaintances at Geneseo, he was becoming a different person.

To all of the affected students of C2D, the meeting with the campus spiritual adviser could not come soon enough.

P.S.S. How did the picture of Tommy come out?!

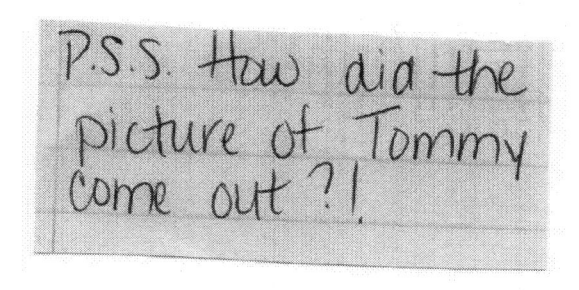

14. DELIVER ME FROM EVIL

While Jeff was balancing his studies with updating his journal, he remembered that he needed to take a roll of film in to be developed. As he reviewed his notes, he recalled that this particular roll was taken on Valentine's Day and contained the photos that were taken in Chris' dorm room during their fledgling investigation. What he was to see when he retrieved the photographs would be something that this small group of friends would remember all their lives.

Jeff, with the envelope containing the recently developed photographs in hand, was conferring with Beth in front of C2D1 as Chris marched tiredly over to them following what was another failed attempt at a long distance run.

"I think I have something interesting to show you, Chris," he said.

"I don't think I want to see them," Chris replied.

Finally, after a few minutes of weak debate, Chris opened the envelope and he and Beth studied the images. Most were only random shots of the dorm room and the items that were in it. Then one peaked Beth's interest, the one that Chris had taken.

"Look at this," she said to Chris.

There in the photo was something that sent a chill through his veins. It was an image of what appeared to be a partially formed *skeleton* floating above his bed and pillows on his side of the loft. Jeff, then Beth, then Chris began to point out -- and verbally name -- the sections of the human skeleton (pelvis, rib cage, spine, and sternum) that were visible in the photograph.

Above - The famous C2D1 Skeletal Image Ghost photograph taken by Chris Di Cesare with J. Jeff Ungar's 35mm camera.

Then silence prevailed as they all sat, numbly staring at the photo. It seemed as if all emotion and feeling had been drained from their bodies.

How could this happen. What is it? They all wondered.

Jeff finally took the photo back and placed it in the envelope.

"I'll need to record the picture in my notes and put it someplace where it will be safe. Where it won't get lost," he said, turning away and heading toward his room.

This photo, of what they understood to be the ghost they had named "Tommy" added significant credibility to the certainty that something paranormal was going on in C2D1.

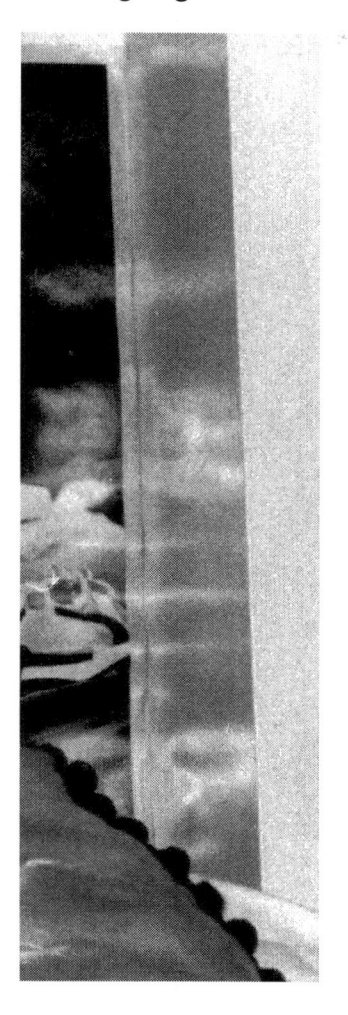

The photograph also added an element of urgency among those most affected by the haunting. Gathering together each evening for a week, the small group discussed what their next step should be in surviving the almost nightly activity. Finally, they all agreed that Paul and Chris would meet with both Father Charlie and Dr. Casler. They also agreed that Paul and Chris would go to the Interfaith Center the next morning while an appointment would be made with Dr. Casler's office as soon as possible.

The ghost's manifestation was once again gaining in strength. It didn't seem the morning could come quite fast enough. As usual, the mischief caused by the entity kept the two dorm mates on edge most of the night; but they somehow managed to get through it in the hope that they would finally meet someone who could help.

Father Charlie Manning's appearance at first startled Chris. He was very young, solidly built, and in some ways looked more like a wrestler than a priest to Chris.

"Can I help you?" he asked.

Chris stated softly that they had been "sent by the church."

"You were sent by the church?" Father Charlie asked, sounding a bit puzzled.

"Oh, no ... we're not *from* the church," Chris immediately blurted out, "We were referred to you BY the church, St. Mary's, up the hill."

"Oh, I understand now. What can I help you with?" asked the priest.

Without hesitation, Chris said, "Well, Father -- we have a ghost in our dorm room and we need your help."

Father Charlie looked at Paul and Chris for a moment, and then said calmly, "Come on in. Want some coffee?"

Chris couldn't help but worry that the priest would think that they were playing some type of joke on him. So after sitting down, he said, "Here -- this is a written account of what has been going on. Just please read the notes first and then let us know what you think."

Father Charlie took Jeff's notes, sat back and began to read. Minutes turned into an hour as he digested every word that had been so meticulously recorded. Occasionally, he would look up at each of the students' faces, perhaps looking for any sign of a ruse; but it was apparent that he was carefully reading each and every word. This made Chris very happy because someone was actually taking them seriously.

Above – Fr. Charlie Manning

At last, when Father Charlie had finished reading, he looked up and closed the journal. Then, taking a deep breath, he said: "I believe you."

Paul and Chris were nearly giddy at the notion that Father Charlie thought that there was indeed something going on in C2D1.

Looking out the window, Father Charlie said, "I definitely believe that there is something going on. I'm not exactly sure what is causing all of this to happen -- but I want to help you."

An enormous wave of relief washed over Chris. After all, Father Charlie might have very well represented his last hope of having a spiritual resolution to the crisis destroying his life.

Then Father Charlie leaned back in his chair and said, "However, I do have a few questions for you first."

The two nodded their acceptance.

"Are you guys doing drugs?"

The question made Chris livid. He was offended by the notion that the priest might think that the activity in C2D1 was caused by the two of them being addicted to drugs, and that he might end up referring them to a rehab program.

"No! I don't do drugs! I can't believe this!" yelled the frustrated Chris.

Not being fazed by the outburst, Father Charlie sat back and calmly said, "Listen, you have to relax. I'm not accusing you of doing drugs. You're coming to me for help. If I try to help you, and it turns out that you were using drugs and I didn't know that, you'd be hurt further and I wouldn't be able to do what I needed to do to help you. Do you both understand?"

Chris and Paul quietly said that they did understand.

"Listen guys, I am asking questions in order to rule a thing out, that's all. Don't take them as accusations."

Chris calmed down while Paul sat complaining to himself that he did not like priests to begin with.

Father Charlie checked his calendar and said "I'll tell you what, I'll be there Wednesday at eight o'clock, and I'll fix your stereo for you."

What the heck is he talking about? Chris wondered, looking at the priest as if he had two heads.

"But, Father, our stereo isn't broken?"

Father Charlie rolled his eyes. "I know that, but I am not going to come in, knock on your dorm hall door and say, 'I'm here to see the ghost.' I read in your notes that you saw the ghost appearing in your stereo; so in case anyone asks, I'm coming in as a stereo repairman."

Oh, man, Chris thought to himself, *this guy has to be the coolest priest ever!*

With renewed confidence, Paul and Chris hoped that all they had to do was survive another two days, and then things would be OK.

Above – A contemporary photograph of the Interfaith Center where in the winter of 1985 Chris and Paul shared Jeff's note with Fr. Charlie Manning.

Leaving the Interfaith Center, Chris felt as if a burden had been lifted from his shoulders. He was elated to know that someone believed that they were truly experiencing something and would help them. Having Father Charlie offer his assistance meant the world to Chris as a person. This was a man of God, and Chris always maintained the hope that there was some Divine Spirit that was beyond the physical. Thinking about the priest's upcoming visit made things seem a little better.

At 8:00 P.M. on Wednesday evening, the phone rang, and Chris was informed that a stereo repairman was looking for him. It was, of course, Father Charlie dressed in a black overcoat and carrying a plain, nondescript briefcase.

Almost in a panic, Chris realized that he had recently hung up a poster of a bikini clad female torso with a martini resting on her hip, and fearing what the priest would think, he quickly ripped it off the wall and threw it into the closet.

Not being a strong believer in anything religious, Paul had gone home as he didn't want any part of what was going to take place.

Father Charlie, led up the stairs by Chris who had met him in Erie Hall's 'C vestibule,' walked into the C2D quad and asked if the first room on the right was the room where the problems were taking place. Chris nodded and the priest entered the room just to look around first. Father Charles slowly took stock of what was in the room, and to Chris, the priest seemed a bit nervous. He noticed that the priest's hands trembled slightly.

Jeff, who had by now become the recognized scribe for the haunting, wanted to be present for the encounter. However, Father Charlie told Jeff that, even though he knew who he was from reading the journal notes, he could not stay in the room. The matter was a personal one for Chris and Paul, not him.

Jeff handed Chris a notebook and pencil instructing him to record everything that was said. And Chris did manage to write a few things down at first, but feeling that it might inappropriate, he stopped recording and focused solely on watching the ritual as it took place.

Chris, thinking it was best to get out of Father Charlie's way, sat down at his desk. The priest pulled out four white candles from his briefcase with the traditional 'IHS' emblazoned on them in red which he then placed, carefully, one in each corner of the room. After lighting each one, he anointed the corners with holy water, then opened his Bible and prayed aloud in each corner. Chris immediately recognized the 'Our Father' and 'Hail Mary' as they were recited, but the third prayer was foreign to him.

Surprisingly, the entire ritual didn't last very long -- perhaps ten or fifteen minutes.

Looking up from his Bible, Father Charlie asked Chris, "Are you all right?"

"I think so," replied Chris.

"Then I believe we're done here," the priest said.

"Uh, wait a second ... what about the exercising?" Chris wondered aloud.

"Do you mean *exorcism?*" asked Father Charlie. "That is only used for when a person is possessed. Are you telling me that you are possessed?"

"Oh, no!" Chris stammered.

"Good. What I did here was a room blessing," Father Charlie explained. "It tells the spirit to find rest, to move on. It informs them that they are no longer welcome in that space anymore and that they need to find a permanent place to rest."

"OK, cool," said Chris.

As Father Charlie was leaving he turned to him and said, "Well

Chris, things should be fine. If you have any more problems just give me a call. Hopefully I'll see you for Sunday services."

Chris was feeling a little disappointed that he had not really experienced anything during the blessing. He had hoped to hear some noise or see something that would tell him, in no uncertain terms, that the ghost had left. All that Chris had was the word of the priest that the entity was now gone. Yet, as a devout Christian he thought Father Charlie should be taken at his word. It was only right to believe him.

And accordingly, he did notice that the room was "quiet." It seemed almost like any other room in the building now, and the oppressive atmosphere that had slowly built up over time seemed gone. Chris wondered if it was the ritual itself or just his imagination. Whatever the case was, the ghost was nowhere to be seen.

Over the next few days, Chris was able to sleep in his room undisturbed. There were no longer any cold breezes, no blinking lights; he saw no shadows, and -- best of all -- no ghost was whispering his name or touching his skin.

After a short time, Chris felt so good that he decided to hold a "Ghost is Gone Party" in his dorm room. Digging out some unused Valentine's Day decorations, Chris and a few of the girls from the B building, went to work getting C2D1 ready for the upcoming celebration.

This feeling of calm would only be short lived, however, as "Tommy" had no intention of leaving. He would now look for someone else connected with Chris in order to regain his attention.

15. ENTER THE WHIRLWIND

For Chris it was important to throw a "Ghost is Gone" party. It would help to compensate for the sheer hell that he had been enduring all semester.

As a competitive athlete, Chris was required to train very hard for his races. But once the race was over, a celebration of some kind was often in order. It didn't matter if he won or not, though he always preferred to, it was more about that feeling of accomplishment that he had when a task was properly completed. Before he left for college, Chris would go out with his family for dinner to help celebrate the moment.

Now he was away from home. But in his mind he was so elated that he had survived what he called his "great spiritual race with the ghost" that he felt it was only appropriate that he celebrate. So, a few days after Father Charlie blessed his room, the celebrants gathered.

For Chris, one of the most important things in life had always been family. And he invited those students who now made up his 'extended family' on campus. Jeff chose not to attend as he had felt that Chris, via Father Charlie, had sent the ghost away before they could understand why it was there in the first place. He felt that they could have learned much more about why the ghost had made his presence known and possibly even who it was

Students who happened to drop by the party were told that it was a late Valentine's Day Party to carefully conceal its real purpose. Being a good host, Chris had all of the mandatory staples of dorm life: chips, beverages and, of course, music.

Surprisingly, Jeff was not the only one who did not show up for the party. After taking a head count, Chris realized that Beth wasn't there, and he decided to go to her room in the B2 quad to see why. He was worried that something had happened to her or that she had become ill.

Erie Hall's three buildings are connected by glass-lined walkways, and Chris wasted no time traversing the halls. Beth's door was partially open when he approached which seemed unusual. Chris yelled in, "Beth, are you OK?"

There was no answer, so he pushed the door completely open with a soft kick and walked in. To his horror, he saw only Beth's bare feet as she lay partially hidden behind her bed on the floor. She was unconscious and the room was in total disarray. Furniture was tipped over and the floor was covered with personal objects.

What happened here? Could she have had a fight with her boyfriend, or even worse, walked in on someone robbing her room?

Chris ran over to her, knelt down and again asked, "Beth! Are you OK? Oh, my God! Wake up, wake up!"

Beth began to come around, and when she was able to speak, told Chris that she had taken a shower and had just come back into her room when she heard his name, "Chris", whispered near her ear. Afraid for her life, she began to throw anything that she could find at the unseen intruder. In her frenzied mind, she thought that if she could only hit it somehow, that it would go away and leave her alone. Beth flailed, knocking over lamps in a vain attempt to drive whatever had spoken to her away. Finally exhausted, she fell to the ground and lost consciousness.

Being ever the chivalrous one, Chris pulled a couple dollars from his pocket and said, "You should get dressed. And, here, get something from the vending machine if you want for the party."

"What about the room?" she asked, sounding quite concerned.

"I'll take care of your room," said Chris.

After he finished putting the room back together, Chris called Jeff from the lounge telephone and described to him what had just discovered. Jeff made a mad dash to where Chris was calling him from. Without Chris even seeing him, he had entered and announced that he was there. He was standing directly behind him which gave Chris quite a fright.

As usual, Jeff had come prepared with all of his equipment hoping to be able to capture any type of evidence. Even so, after a short amount of time, they both decided that it would be best to return back to the C2D quad and for Chris to rejoin the party.

Chris was still anguished seeing his friend lying on the floor of her dorm room and he knew what the reality of the situation was: "Tommy," who had been forced to leave C2D1 during the blessing, was now searching for Chris by targeting those closest to him. In fact, Linda, who was another friend of Chris' and whose dorm room was several doors down from Beth's also had visits by the ghost. She reported being touched on her leg by someone that she couldn't see and having the feeling that someone was pressing down on top of her when she was alone in her room. She, too, claimed to hear Chris' name being whispered in her ear.

Above – Amazing photograph by Jeff Ungar of Linda and Chris, as he attempts to 'feel' for the ghost that she claimed had been holding her down in her bed.

What Chris soon comprehended was that the ghost was visiting everyone he knew, showing up in the rooms that he would frequent the most whenever he left his own. The blessing of his room which he had at first heralded as a miracle, was now something that seemed to be quickly transforming into a curse instead.

What was now foremost on his mind was the thought that the ghost would harm his college family in order to get to him. Ultimately, he reasoned, it did not say either of the girl's names -- it had whispered his.

No longer was Chris confident that the blessing of his room had been totally effective. Chris knew that he needed to take responsibility for what was going on. But what could he do? The situation was becoming far more complicated than he ever could have imagined.

To make matters worse, events were now beginning to be reported around the campus. What students once whispered about in their darkened dorm rooms now was discussed out in the open. Rumors and the college's urban legends began to take on new lives and spread like wildfire. In the college library, the dining hall, outside dorm room windows, "Tommy the Ghost" seemed to be everywhere.

Many of Chris' inner-circle continued to experience phenomena. Disembodied voices, cold spots and dark shadows darted across their rooms as they studied. Perhaps even more disconcerting was the fact that word had now spread that a student in Erie Hall had a ghost 'living' in his dorm room!

There seem to be nowhere to hide. As Chris was sitting with a group of friends in the dining hall, a female student he did not recognize actually pointed at him. Then he overheard her say, "Look, that's the Ghost Boy!"

Turning to Jeff, he said, "Did you hear that?" Jeff affirmed that he did indeed and the two of them took what was left of their food and went to eat in the quiet of their rooms. As they ate, Chris made Jeff promise to try to protect him from any notoriety that might come as a result of his interaction with "Tommy." Chris was worried that this type of attention being focused on him might tarnish his family's name, and to him, that was an intolerable thought.

A few days later while he was walking by the administration building, he overheard two students watching a small TV crew that was in town doing a follow up to a campus rumor that was circulating about a boy who saw ghosts. Chris narrowly avoided them by ducking behind a mailbox and waiting until the disappointed reporters climbed into their van and drove away.

The haunting of Erie Hall was becoming big news, and had, in fact, spilled over to the point where after a short run, Chris saw a reporter standing outside of the dorm interviewing any student who would talk to him about stories of the ghost. Chris ducked behind a bush near the sidewalk and stayed there until he saw the reporter snap a few pictures and eventually walk away.

All of this unwanted attention was beginning to wear Chris thin. Life as he remembered it to be was still not back in his grasp, nor did it look like it would be possible to feel normal again. It seemed as though the world was turning upside down, and Chris, for all his efforts, had no power to stop it.

16. WHEN THE DEAD COME CALLING

By March, Chris was beginning to suffer greatly because of the oppressive atmosphere that was swirling around him. He knew that his father would be upset to learn that he had stopped running for the college and his mother would definitely become concerned that his grades were now worse than ever. When he had tried to resolve matters through his faith, it did not work. Reaching hard to find a logical answer, he realized there was none.

Chris also tried to work through the situation with his roommate Paul, and was told by him in no indefinite terms that he was going to leave and not come back if things didn't get any better.

Worse, his friends were now being influenced by the ghost in a negative way. Chris felt as if he were standing on the edge of an abyss. On one side were darkness and the overwhelming feeling of depression, and on the other side, the leering dead eyes of the ghost.

For Chris, there was only one thing to do: try to get back on track with his one practical passion: running.

Chris had to force himself to go through the all too familiar motions that he needed to get past the first mile. As the road whisked by, his body finally clicked onto autopilot and the miles began melting away. Up ahead was a familiar sight: an historic marker proclaiming the area to be a Revolutionary War Era site called 'The Torture Tree.' Not being a big fan of Revolutionary War history (he tended to side -- in principle -- with the Loyalists) he never paid much attention to it. To him, it was simply another distance marker, letting him know approximately how far he had run.

Having made the valiant effort to get out there and run, Chris returned back to Erie Hall with a clearer head. Now it was time to take a shower. He had long since stopped being afraid to shower in the C2D quad. After all, his room had been blessed.

Closing the big wooden roller door of the bathroom behind him, Chris hung his towel on the hook and stepped into the shower stall.

As he shampooed his hair, he looked up and saw a giant black shadow move from left to right.

Whoa, are you kidding me? Chris thought. *Oh, man. I'm freaking myself out. It's probably nothing. I must have rubbed some soap into my eyes,* he rationalized.

But then he became a bit apprehensive, thinking about what had happened in both Beth and Linda's rooms.

Suddenly, the shadow crossed again, but this time from right to left.

Geez! He thought, *either the ghost is in here or someone snuck into the bathroom while I was turning on the water.* Slowly stepping out from the shower stall, Chris called out, "Hello, is anyone here?"

There was no reply; so he stepped back into the shower to rinse his hair and then he planned on beating a hasty retreat back to the safety of his room. After all ... nothing was going on there anymore ... *right?*

Just as he reached for the lever and turned the water off, Chris felt a burning pain in his back.

What the hell just happened?! It was as if someone had pressed a hot poker to his skin and it immediately took his breath away.

Whatever had touched him had felt sharp and had struck fast. Crying out in pain, Chris turned to face the shower stall opening and swung out with a clenched fist hoping to catch whoever was there in the face. He figured that if his assailant still had a weapon, he would most likely lose, but he intended to go down fighting anyway.

Ripping the shower curtain from the rod that held it, Chris lashed out, but the only thing his fist connected with was the curtain itself.

With adrenaline pumping through his veins, he stood for a few moments in the center of the small bathroom.

"Who are you?! What do you want?! " Chris screamed, "Who are you? ... God? ... The Devil? ... Come and talk to me, you coward! Show yourself!"

Catching his reflection in the mirror over the three sinks, he saw blood trickling down his back.

Oh, my God. Are you kidding me? My back is bleeding! He thought incredulously, and then dropped to the floor.

Above – Close-up of the shower stall inside the bathroom of the D quad of Erie Hall where, on March 19th, 1985, Di Cesare was viciously attacked.

Chris could feel the cold floor tiles on which he was lying press against the front of his body. He watched intently as a single drop of water rolled, ever so slowly, down his arm and then darkened the grout between two floor tiles. He fought the urge to just let go and pass out. Then he heard the sound of footsteps approaching. Sliding the door open, Jeff looked down and yelled, "Are you all right?" Chris didn't answer.

Jeff grabbed the closest towel and wrapped it around Chris' waist, then helped him up off the floor, across the hall and into his dorm room.

As Chris sat silently at the foot of Jeff's bed, Jeff looked for the source of the blood. Three deep scratches were now etched on

Chris' back from torso to shoulder. Two were very long, one being close to his spine and another starting at his shoulder going downward. The third one was just left of his spine but much shorter than the rest -- its painful looking curves gave the impression that it had been done by the thumb of a hand with only three sharp claws.

Above – Photograph taken from room C2D2, the room of Jeff and Ed. This was the view that Chris had, gazing out the window, as Jeff and Beth carefully tended to the wounds on his back.

Jeff's roommate, Ed, who had been distant to Chris during this entire ordeal, came in and saw Chris' bleeding back and said, "Oh, my God ... oh, my God. This *is* real, isn't it."

Chris sniped back, "Do I get my purple heart now, Ed?"

Grabbing a bottle of hydrogen peroxide from a first aid kit, Jeff gently cleaned the wounds causing Chris to wince in pain.

Then the young man who had gone through so much, limped quietly to his room, crawled onto his loft and fell fast asleep.

17. A FATHER'S LOVE

March in Geneseo, New York, can be a sullen and reflective time. The snowfall is moderate and the temperatures will slowly rise, giving way to the muddy green pastures of April. Chris gave little notice to the season as he numbly attended classes.

Everyday activities that he once enjoyed had become pure drudgery. Even attending Sunday services at St. Mary's was now less important than it had once been. The attack in the shower had left him with scars that were far deeper than what could be seen on his skin.

On March 12th, Jeff and Chris were sitting in the quad's common room talking about the latest campus news, when Chris noticed that something seemed to be deeply hidden within the branches of the tree just outside of the window he was facing. Slowly his eyes adjusted and a form seemed to take shape. It seemed to have been intertwined within the leaves, seemingly the very fiber of the tree itself. Then, to his revulsion, he saw the shape of "Tommy" looking back at him.

Up until now, the ghost had revealed itself in the same shape, time and again; however, this time something was different. Chris felt as if his entire body was being pushed back into the chair on which he sat. "Tommy's" body appeared terribly mutilated. The ghost's eye hung from its socket by the sinew that once allowed it to move. Two dark holes were now in the place where the nose used to be. Its ears were missing and what looked like strips of flesh hung from its chest and arms. What horrified Chris the most was that there was a gaping cut in the lower part of its stomach and what looked to be intestines hanging out. Dark red blood seemed to cover every inch of the specter's body, and Chris could do nothing but stare.

As suddenly as the vision had come, it disappeared. Chris quickly darted out of the room, yelling, "Oh, my God! Jeff, that was horrible! Why would it do that? Why would it look like that to me? What was wrong with it?" Jeff had seen nothing.

After this unsettling incident there seemed no one else to turn to. Chris, fearing the worst, picked up the phone and called his father to make plans to come home for St. Patrick's Day.

The visit home was a welcome relief for Chris. There in the warmth of his family he could finally rest knowing that he was safe and secure. His mother made mention that while he still looked like the same person who had left for college only a few months before, he now seemed like a totally different person. She asked, "What happened to you? Why aren't you the person that you used to be?" She did make sure, however, that he knew she would always love him -- no matter what.

His father commented that he looked a bit too thin and gaunt and told him to take more vitamins. In actuality, Chris had lost almost 20 pounds, something that a person with low body fat could not afford to do. Little could they imagine what was really going on at the sleepy Finger Lakes campus.

Back in Geneseo, Paul was facing a horrible reality. He was still experiencing unexplainable activity in C2D1 even though Chris claimed that the priest had driven the ghost away. To Paul's way of thinking, the situation had become totally unmanageable.

It was well known that Paul was spending less and less time in C2D quad and had even been driving the long distance home on weekends. He had suffered through "Tommy's" earlier mischief and endured the sleepless nights watching the ghost hovering near his loft. Most recently, he walked into the dorm room only to find one of his notebooks floating in mid-air. The final straw was when he heard the gravelly whisper of "Tommy" telling him to "leave Chris alone."

Even though a few days earlier Jeff had agreed to change rooms with him, Paul did not feel as if he was ever going to be safe in the quad.

By the time Chris returned to Erie Hall after his visit home, Jeff was already beginning to move a few of his things into C2D1. Paul informed Chris of the room change and Chris seemed to be happy at the prospect of now sharing his room with someone who would support him. Everyone went to bed that night feeling more relaxed, except for Paul.

Unfortunately, he had already hit his breaking point: the next morning -- without a word -- Paul went home. He quickly withdrew from school and never returned, leaving most of his books, furniture, and clothing behind.

Chris felt somewhat betrayed by Paul's sudden departure, but at the same time he looked forward to the future. After all, he felt safe with Jeff in the same room with him. For Jeff, however, his first evening in C2D1 was far from being uneventful.

In the middle of a sound sleep, he was awoken by a pressure on his chest. He could move his arms just a little, but the rest of his body seemed almost paralyzed and held in place by a shadowy figure that was kneeling directly on his chest. Struggling for release, Jeff finally was able to break free sending the ghost into the air from which it evaporated into the night. Not wishing to alarm Chris, and knowing that the ghost was 'technically' off limits because of the blessing that had taken place, he chose not to tell Chris about the experience.

The uproar that was caused by "Tommy" continued throughout the weeks that led up to Chris' birthday which was March 31st. That year, the date was also shared by the Christian holiday of Palm Sunday.

Returning home for his birthday, his parents now noticed just how thin he had actually become. They were alarmed, but Chris passed off his weight loss to academic stress. After another restful weekend away from "Tommy" and all those others who were seeking the "Ghost Boy," Chris felt that through sheer willpower he could finish out the semester. Making his way back to the Geneseo campus, Chris walked sullenly into Erie Hall once again.

After a few hours in the dorm, Chris began to feel uneasy and the world around him seemed to whirl out of control. He was having difficulty breathing, and every sound that was made echoed loudly in his head. A wave of panic washed over him, and for the first time in his life he thought that he might be dying. He wondered if the ghost was killing him.

Above – Di Cesare, appearing very gaunt, made one trip home during the months of the haunting, to celebrate his 20th birthday with his family.

Chris made his way to the telephone and placed a frantic call to his father. Hearing the voice of the only person whom Chris felt could save him from his own demise, he spilled out details of the haunting which he had so carefully hidden from him.

"Dad, I'm in big trouble," said Chris.

"What? Why?" his father asked.

"Dad, I have to talk to you about something."

"Well what is it Chris? You can tell me anything, and you know that."

"Dad, there is a ghost up here -- I'm being haunted. It won't leave me alone! I think I should come back home."

There were a few moments of dead air as Vito Di Cesare collected his thoughts.

"Come on now, be reasonable. This isn't funny. You know college is expensive, and you just can't go back if you quit. You know you are making a foolish mistake if you leave. Chris, are you all right? Are you taking some kind of drug?

"Dad you have to believe me. It's been happening for over a month. I don't know if I can take it anymore," Chris blurted out.

Always looking for a logical explanation to any problem, Vito said, "I'll tell you what. You and Jeff go out to the athletic field and find three of the biggest guys that you can. You get them to come back to your dorm room and see what happens. I'll stay on the line."

So, off Chris and Jeff went to find several rugby players who came back under the assumption that there was a sort of party going on.

Accompanying them back the room and seeing no party, one of them asked, "What's going on?"

Chris said "Hold on, just wait a few seconds."

Within moments, the biggest of the three jumped up and screamed, "What's on my leg? Oh, my God. Something just grabbed my leg!"

It was as if a bolt of electricity filled the room.

They all jumped up screaming and literally ran out of the room.

Chris came back to the telephone and said "Dad ... " with his voice trailing off.

"I'm on my way," said Mr. Di Cesare.

After a five hour drive from Orange County, N.Y., to Geneseo, Vito Di Cesare arrived at Erie Hall. He was tired but his son mattered more than his own exhaustion. Chris met him at the door and together they went to C2D1.

Chris was in a state of panic as he told him more details of the haunting. Mr. Di Cesare calmed him with words that only a loving father could say and assured him that he would stand guard as he slept that night.

Mr. Di Cesare may have been someone who needed scientific proof, but he was no fool. As he sat in the darkened room, he took no chances. With him, he had brought a baseball bat and a handgun. Since Jeff had gone home for the weekend, there was room for Chris' father to comfortably stay in C2D1. Whatever was going on there, father and son would deal with it together.

As the long night passed, Mr. Di Cesare listened to the rhythmic sound of Chris' breathing as he slept. Sitting at the foot of the loft, he was determined to 'stand guard' for the remainder of the night.

In the murky dark, he began to feel an overwhelming presence that seemed to be emanating from the closet. In the darkness, Mr. Di Cesare watched as the closet door slowly opened a few inches. Standing there was a shadow. For a man who had prized common sense and logic his entire life, this was an enigma. For the very first time he felt that perhaps he did not want to know what was in there.

As dawn broke, Chris awoke from his slumber. His father had not slept the entire night. Mr. Di Cesare pondered how he could help his son through this insane situation. Being pragmatic and having an unswerving faith, he instinctively knew that the solution "had to come from within Chris himself."

Also, so as not to frighten Chris any more than he already was, his father decided not to tell him of his own experiences. Pulling on his sneakers, Vito suggested that the two of them go for a run around the campus which would provide both father and son a chance to clear their heads about what was currently going on.

When they got back to the dorm, Chris' father looked directly into his eyes and said, "You know that you can always turn to me. You can turn to your mother. If you need help, just call. And, Chris … move out of this room!"

Then he reached into his bag he pulled out the crucifix that he had received from his grandmother which contained a small vial of holy water that was placed into a hollowed notch in its back surface.

"Keep it close by," he warned. "Also, when you get the chance you go to your "RD" (Dormitory Resident Director) and get another room. Promise me that you will."

Chris said that he would, and Mr. Di Cesare hugged his son and began the long return trip. When he arrived back at home, Chris' father sent him a letter:

> A PERSON ENTERING A FIELD THAT MIGHT DEAL WITH EMOTIONALLY DISTURBED INDIVIDUALS MUST BE A PARAGON OF STABILITY. YOU SHOULD BE THE PERSON THAT OTHERS SEEK INFORMATION FROM. WHATEVER YOU MIGHT BELIEVE OTHERS WILL DEAL WITH YOUR INFORMATION IN A SKEPTICAL WAY UNLESS THEY ** FEEL   SEE   TOUCH ** THOSE THINGS YOU DO. IF THEY DO NOT, YOU AVAIL YOURSELF TO CRITICISM OF STABILTY, NOW ON THE OTHER HAND A BRIEF NOTE ON PHILOSOPHY--TO SEEK IS TO FIND. TO DENY IS TO ADMIT THAT THERE MAY BE, THUS , SEEK AND YE SHALL FIND THOSE THINGS THAT DO NOT EXIST, FOR YOU SHALL CREATE THEM IN SPIRIT OR FORM, IN REAL OR IN MIND; AND IF IT IS ALIVE AND EXISTING IN MIND, THEREFORE IT WILL BE REAL FOR YOU, EVEN IF NOT FOR ANYONE ELSE. BELIEF THEREFORE IS THE KEY.
>
> I AM ALIVE NOW IN YOUR MIND AS YOU READ THIS. BUT DO YOU KNOW OTHER THAN FAITH OR BELIEF? AND IF YOU READ THIS 50 YEARS FROM NOW WHEN I AM DEAD WILL I EXIST ANY MORE OR LESS THAN THE WAY I EXIST IN YOUR MIND NOW? DO NOT BELIEVE AND I DO NOT EXIST, BELIEVE AND I DO.

A few days later, as he had promised his dad, Chris stopping by the "RD's" office and inquired if he could change his room and he was told, once again, in no uncertain terms: "No." There were only four weeks left in the semester and he had no other choice but to tough it out.

Later that day, Craig N., Jeff's former roommate from a previous semester, approached Chris and admitted that he had overheard his conversation with his father.

"Listen," he said, "Just so that you know, one of the guys in the other suite is claiming that he might have a ghost in his room. I think it might be calling your name. It's freaking him out. You want to check it out?"

Feeling that he already had enough to deal with, Chris said, "No, I don't" and left it at that.

"Tommy" seemed to be gaining even more strength and became more unruly throughout the month.

By the beginning of April, the girls were all reporting more activity in their dorm rooms. This angered Chris to no end. It was one thing to attack him -- that he could almost deal with -- but to be bothering innocent people was, in his mind, totally unacceptable. He hated what was going on and vowed to do something about it. It was the emergence of these fierce emotions that seemed to rekindle the spark within him that had been snuffed out by the constant stress of dealing with the spirit.

Chris' body once again began to grow stronger and the dullness that his mind was experiencing began to dissipate. Chris felt that it was time to slowly awaken from the nightmare.

18. PROOF AT LAST

It was obvious that Jeff and Chris needed to explore other avenues of attack against the onslaught of "Tommy's" harassment. It had grown apparent that in order to get rid of the ghost, they would need to try to find out what it wanted.

When Paul and Chris had originally met with Father Charlie, they had blown off the appointment with Dr. Lawrence Casler that Beth had made. Dr. Casler was a Psychology Professor with whom Beth had taken a class. Perhaps, they reasoned, the recommendations of someone familiar with the study of psychology and parapsychology might be able to shed more light on their problems.

This course of action really appealed to Jeff right away as he had always felt that a scientific approach might be more effective in the long run. However, he warned Chris: "Parapsychologists observe and study, so I don't want to get your hopes up. I mean he's not going to come into Erie Hall with some kind of meter and blow the ghost up like in the movies. He's going to want to determine things." Chris, who just wanted to get rid of the ghost simply said,

"Whatever, Jeff ... fine. If he can help in any way, let's go."

So, in early April, Beth, Jeff and Chris visited the teaching office of Dr. Casler. He admitted that he had grown concerned when they failed to keep their initial February appointment. However, he freely admitted that in the field of parapsychology these things happened more frequently than most people think. Back in 1985, though, there was still a stigma associated with anything to do with the paranormal. While the subject did make for a few thought provoking debates, it simply wasn't accepted in many scholastic circles.

After Beth introduced her two friends to the professor, she walked to the back of the room and sat down. Dr. Casler motioned for Jeff and Chris to sit down closer to his desk. Chris sized him up. He seemed to be an intellectual person. There was something in the way that he spoke, the way that he dressed. He looked just like what Chris imagined a real scholar would look like. Dr. Casler was also well traveled, having been all across the globe, looking for places where the supernatural crossed paths with science.

After hearing the story of "Tommy," he appeared stunned by the fact that right there on his back doorstep, so to speak, unexplainable phenomena were taking place.

Chris was excited by the fact that Dr. Casler seemed to know far more about the subject than he or Jeff could ever realize. He suggested that Jeff and Chris go back to Erie Hall and attempt to establish communication with the ghost and perhaps even use a cassette recorder to capture the sounds that it made. In this way they might discover why "Tommy" was focused upon C2D1 and on Chris.

Chris mentioned that the ghost had made gurgling and hissing sounds when he heard it, so there was a possibility that they might be able to capture that on tape as well.

Toward the end of the meeting, Dr. Casler said to Chris, "Before you leave, I would like to speak to you in private. Just you. You seem to have a certain skill set, certain aspects of your personality that intrigue me. And as the ghost is focusing on you, I feel that I should, too. So, maybe I can set an appointment, and we can meet sometime."

Chris made the appointment, wondering in the back of his mind just what they were going to talk privately about.

The three friends returned to Erie Hall and attempted to "hunt" for "Tommy" by tape recorder. Linda had sent word that her books had been moved and that she had heard whispers again in her dorm room. Jeff, Chris and Beth immediately rushed over there. It was Jeff's job to secure the room and check for anything that could possibly make any type of noise. He locked all the windows and made sure that her closet door and desk were secured. When all was ready, Chris set the tape recorder on the desk and he began to talk.

"Hello, Tommy" said Chris apprehensively. "I kept my promise, I'm here. I'm trying to help you. If you'd like to say anything, I'm leaving this box on, right here … for approximately fifteen minutes. All you have to do is speak. It will pick up your voice. At a later time, I can rewind the tape and hear what you said. In this way I can speak to you. I'll come back tomorrow around the same time, if you have left any questions for me, I'll answer them. If you have any statements, I'll ask you about them. As I said, I'm trying to help. In order to help, I must know what your purpose is and why you are here. I hope you understand."

Jeff then gave Chris the room key and he walked out locking the door behind him. He then took a chair and wedged it under the doorknob so it could not be opened and sat down in front of it so no one could get in. Jeff, having set himself up as 'room guardian,' re-checked that the door was locked and secured, looked up at Chris and nodded his satisfaction. Chris, already tense with anxiety, decided to go back to C2D1 for a short while in order to avoid any physical contact with the ghost. He put Linda's room key into a pocket and walked away. Beth and Linda offered to accompany him, to which Chris replied: "Sure, if you want to."

Jeff then synchronized his wrist watch with Chris' and reminded him not to be late in returning.

Once in his room, the two ladies tried to lighten the mood a bit. They both cared deeply for Chris and they hated seeing how the haunting had taken his once upbeat personality away. Very quickly, Beth and Linda initiated an informal game of truth or dare which soon found numerous pieces of clothing scattered across the room. Chris, who was at first strongly resistant to the idea found the accompanying exuberance and laughter simply too hard to battle. He hadn't laughed this hard in over a month.

Thirty-five minutes quickly passed. Chris, by now wearing only a broad smile and a pair of running shorts on his head, glanced over at his watch to check the time.

"Oh, no! Jeff is going to be furious at me!" He yelled out to the girls. They had lost track of the time. Chaos quickly ensued as they began the process of locating all of their clothing.

Reaching Linda's dorm room they all saw Jeff pacing back and forth.

"Where were you?" Jeff asked.

Chris made an attempt to create a meaningful alibi, but Jeff, focused in the critical task at hand, cut him off: "Let's see what was recorded!"

Together, they unlocked and opened the door, and sure enough, they found that the tape recorder had been moved along with the desk chair. *Oh no, it was here,* Chris thought to himself.

Jeff couldn't conceal his satisfaction that something had happened in a controlled environment. Pressing the stop button and rewinding the tape, they all gathered around the desk to listen. Disappointingly, all that greeted their ears was the common 'hiss' that all cassette decks made when recording dead air.

Ten, then fifteen minutes passed. Chris, his mind still reflecting on the fun time he just had with Beth and Linda thought to himself: *Wow, this is so boringly weird! Here I am in college, with these two pretty girls right next to me, and we are all sitting on the floor listening to static for half an hour.*

In that moment Chris realized how much the haunting was truly transforming his life.

Suddenly, strange noises were heard on the tape. It sounded as if a chair had been dragged across the linoleum tile floor. Then what sounded to all of them like some sort of heavy breathing: whatever had made that sound must have stood right by the tape recorder! They were all excited and amazed until they heard the next sound: it was like a low moaning voice. Chris and the girls were instantly creeped out by it, but Jeff clenched his fist and ecstatically chopped at the air saying, "Yes!"

Finally, he was hearing something, and it had been recorded in a room that he himself had secured. He knew that combined with the first person accounts and the photographs, this was definitely a strong case. *This just might be a way to communicate directly with the ghost and learn more about the paranormal and life after death*, Jeff thought excitedly.

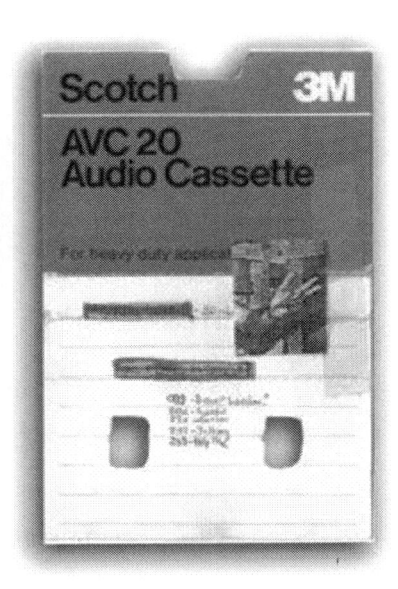

Above – The cassette tape and cassette tape cover from the "Ghost Tape" recorded in the girl's suite in 1985.

Chris' reaction was the polar opposite of Jeff's. *What have I done?* he questioned himself, horrified, *I've offered to help this thing if it talked to me, and now I have a verbal contract with it! I can't look at, I can't face, AND it attacked me!*

While Chris pondered what would happen next, Jeff said he was going to bring the tape up to the college music lab and speed it up and slow it down in order to try to hear if he can make out any words or phrases.

"OK," Chris blankly replied, as he walked out of room B2B2, hoping never to have to go back in there. When he arrived in his room, he lowered himself onto his knees, closed his eyes and prayed to God for the courage to move forward. He doubted that he had it. He then took a scalding hot shower that turned his skin pink as he tried unsuccessfully to 'wash away' the sounds of the ghost's voice that he had heard on the tape: *'Chris ... help! Help me, Chris!'*

The remainder of the night was uneventful. The next morning, Jeff went off to class and Chris stopped by Dr. Casler's office, keeping his appointment.

Dr. Casler was very happy to see him, almost like a child on Christmas morning. In Chris' mind, he wondered why Dr. Casler was so excited because he was only bringing him what he felt was a serious problem. But for Dr. Casler, this was a chance to work in real time with someone currently experiencing unexplained events. Who knew what he might uncover!

"Now, Chris, I'd like you to sit down so we can do an exercise or two. I have in front of me a deck of Zener cards. They are not playing cards and have no numbers, just shapes and colors. Now I am going to take the first card off the top of the deck; I'm going to look at it, put it to my forehead, and visualize what I saw on the front of the card. I want you to tell me what card you think I am visualizing."

Chris looked at him like he was speaking another language.

"Look, Dr. Casler ... I'm sorry, I can't do that. I have no clue what you're looking for. This is embarrassing to me, sir. I'm going to fail, and I feel like I've failed enough this semester."

"Fair enough," Dr. Casler replied, "but humor me and let's just do a few. If nothing happens we'll simply stop."

Chris begrudgingly agreed.

Dr. Casler then described what was on the cards. There would be wavy lines, a box, a star, and different other shapes.

"Now, Chris, concentrate."

Chris, humoring him, blurted out the first thing that came to mind: "Wavy lines."

"OK, next one."

"A square," Chris replied.

Dr. Casler pulled five more cards and said, "Chris you're doing very well, keep going!"

After the last card in the deck was pulled, he looked up and said, "I have some news for you. You got every single one wrong."

"See? I told you that I wasn't going to be good at this," said Chris his voice cracking.

"You don't understand, Chris. It is almost impossible for a person to get every single one wrong. The 'Law of Averages' says that you should get at least some right. However, this is what is so unusual -- with every card except two you were able to name the card that was still face down on the table, not the one that I was actually holding. What you did is called a 'Positive One Step Progression!' I believe that this may be why the ghost is talking to you. Biologically you seem to possess a sensitivity that it can relate to. To the ghost you are much like a 'vacancy' sign outside a motel that invites it to come on in. Imagine a neon sign that is bright and loud! Now, you need to understand that these things may very well happen to you for the rest of your life."

At that news, Chris stood up, thanked Dr. Casler for his time, and told him that he didn't want to be late for his next class.

"Let's talk some more in the near future." Dr. Casler added.

Rattled by the results of the experiment and by Dr. Casler's reaction, Chris left the basement office and never went back. Chris' goal was put an end to the events in C2D1 as soon as possible. Dr. Casler saying that he would have this type of phenomena happen to him the rest of his life freaked him out, and in his mind he knew that he wouldn't be able to deal with it.

19. THE CONFRONTATION

After the success of the tape experiment in Linda's room, Chris now understood that "Tommy" would respond to him, and what he was asking for: help. There had been several times when the ghost was in Chris' room, and it seemed to be trying to say something, but no sound could be heard. Chris had seen "Tommy's" lips move several times, but only blood would trickle from the corners of his mouth as if forced out from damaged lungs. Before the tape, Chris had begun to lose hope that he would ever understand why the ghost had chosen him out of all the students on campus to trouble.

Chris' life was still in turmoil. In the process of slowly regaining his confidence, he was still reeling from what was going on around him. Jeff wanted to continue to proceed, with caution, onto additional organized experiments. Chris, on the other hand, just wanted to be done with the entire episode and get his life back on track. Those terrible thoughts he had of simply 'giving up' were gradually beginning to fade away.

In his mind, however, the only option he could see that remained for him to do was to leave school. If indeed he really was the epicenter of the haunting as Dr. Casler had suggested, then leaving would be the only way he could truly hope to protect his friends. He just didn't know yet how he would explain that choice to his already worried parents.

Enter Craig.

Craig Norris was very imposing both in personality and action. It seemed, at times, as if he was a beardless carbon copy of Jeff: but where Jeff was introverted, Craig was extremely outgoing. He was one of those individuals who said what he had to say regardless of who attempted to dominate the conversation. His brilliant and forceful personality greatly intimidated Chris. Oftentimes, Craig would see someone walking across the lobby talking with a friend and he would quickly interject himself into the conversation that they were having. He kept abreast of what was going on in the world of politics, the environment and history.

Craig had once told Chris never to walk to class the same way every day because he wouldn't "learn anything new." He was just so different and counter-cultural that he frankly scared the hell out of the regulated and well-organized Chris!

As was his custom, Craig had been observing the goings on in the C2D quad. He could not help but notice the turmoil that the roommates seemed to be in. Chris, the focused runner, was now too thin to be effective on the track. Paul had already left, and the rumors flying around Erie Hall about ghosts were, by that point, common knowledge. In Craig's mind, there was only one thing that could end this turmoil, and that was to tell Chris exactly what he thought should be done.

It was four o'clock in the morning, and Chris having awoken from a horrific nightmare in which all of his friends were slowly dying, opted to take a cold shower to wash the experience from his mind. Craig was already in the bathroom shaving while wearing sunglasses. Chris immediately decided not to ask why.

As Chris quietly took his shower, Craig saw his opportunity. He pulled the shower curtain open, positioned his face an inch from Chris' and -- in no uncertain terms -- told Chris: "You've got to stop running from yourself! And not only from yourself, but you've also got to stop running from your responsibilities, and from this thing, whatever it is! Go into your dorm room and talk to it; you've got to deal with it. Otherwise, my friend, things are definitely not going to get any better."

Chris who was standing there awkwardly naked in front of this forceful individual attempted to regain some sense of privacy, but Craig would not let Chris backslide.

"Listen, you don't have a choice. If you don't do this, you're going to run from everything in your life. This is your chance to become the person you're supposed to be. You can't rely on other people to do things for you. Your dad isn't going to help you; the priest is not going to help you; and the press isn't going to help you. You have to help yourself, my friend!"

"Wait. Are you saying this thing is some type of poltergeist?" Chris asked worriedly.

"I don't know what this thing is, Chris. Jeff thinks it might be a lost spirit that you brought home with you after one of your long runs; Paul thinks that it is the ghost of a dead boy who has its sights trained on you. But it doesn't matter *what* it is! You are suffering! Your friends are suffering! Please realize that these people need you."

Visibly shaken by his outburst, Chris looked at him sadly and said, "You're right. I'll do it."

"Right now?" asked Craig.

"Yes," Chris replied, "right now."

Chris turned off the running water and reached for his shorts to cover up his nakedness.

"No," said Craig, "You're going in the way that God made you."

"Really?" Chris stammered.

"Yes, with no pretense and no lies -- just the honest you!" Craig commanded. "You go in the way God made you. You bare both body and soul to that thing. Talk to it, and get this done."

"Alright," said Chris, who then walked out of the bathroom and into C2D1 to face whatever outcome would happen.

Once inside his room, Chris nervously searched for a candle and placed it in the middle of the floor. His body shook with fear. Kneeling down, he recited the "Our Father" and "Hail Mary" just as Father Charlie had done. He then began praying to God that even if the ghost was to hurt or kill him that night, at least everything would end there.

Chris could feel water dripping off of his still shivering body as he did not have the time to dry off from his shower. "OK, Tommy, here I am. This is it. If you want my help, then I'm here for you; but you have to come now. I have the strength and the courage to be here, so please do this now. If you don't come now, I can never help you. Please, talk with me."

Above – The area above the loft in room C2D1 of Erie Hall.

Then, in the silence, Chris knelt and again prayed. The flickering candle was the only source of light in the room. He kept his hips turned slightly towards the door in the event that he would have to attempt to run.

Minutes passed and nothing happened. Chris was somewhat relieved, of course, but at the same time was thinking that this torture might never end.

As before, though, Chris soon began to feel that familiar drop in temperature. It was as if a cold breeze was gently blowing from behind him. It chilled his already cold body further. Looking up and to his right, he could see a black, human-shaped shadow glide unevenly past his desk. Fear slowly began to overtake him as he knew that the ghost was beginning to manifest in his room. He stood up, trembling from fear and cold, and closed his eyes tightly hoping that if he could not see the ghost, it might not be able to harm him. Then something strange in the room caught his attention. It smelled like he had stuck his head into an ice cream freezer.

Opening his eyes, Chris saw that the apparition was standing there, right in front of him, looking at him. This time, he decided that as horrifying as it might be, that he would attempt to look directly into "Tommy's" face. It was then he saw that there were tears running down its face from those unblinking eyes. Chris then saw that "Tommy" was attempting to speak, without much success. Choking and gasping sounds were all that he could make out.

Above – Representation of the "Tommy" the C2D1 Ghost, as created by Chris Di Cesare, in order to help illustrate its appearance.

And something else was very unusual, too: "Tommy" was standing before him totally naked just like Chris was.

Finally, in what must have been a supreme effort, "Tommy" uttered in a low voice: "Wrong, so wrong … so much pain."

To Chris these words were said in pure anguish and suffering.

Chris had never witnessed anything so heartbreaking in his life and for the first time felt empathy for the pitiful creature that now stood before him.

Pushing his emotions aside, Chris found his voice and said, "Look, Tommy, you have to understand that people love you no matter what you did. You have to find forgiveness. You have to know that you are OK, and you have to find rest for yourself."

The ghost made a gurgling sound and blood seemed to leak from its mouth. Tears welled up in Chris' eyes as he continued, "You have to accept that things will be OK. You have to let go; you can't stay here. You're hurting my friends, you're hurting me, and you're taking away my very will to live. And if you do that, you will never find any rest. So you need to close your eyes and open up your soul and embrace God, or whatever is out there. You have to go. You can't stay here anymore."

At that moment the candle flame flickered wildly and Chris quickly glanced down at the floor by his feet, hoping that the room's tan carpet had not caught fire.

Looking back up, he saw that the thing that had caused so much torment in his life ... was seemingly gone.

The following day, when Jeff arrived back at C2D1, he could feel the change in the room. For him, even after the blessing, there had always seemed to be a hint of foreboding. Now it was airy and light, much like the other quad rooms on the floor.

Looking over at Chris, he saw a person that was as relaxed and as jovial as he knew him to be before "Tommy" had taken center stage in his life.

Chris was hesitant to share what had happened just a few hours earlier, and Jeff felt that it was not his place to push the issue.

That night, April 20th, 1985, the entire population of Erie Hall would sleep peacefully for the first time in many weeks.

20. THE WORLD TODAY

On April 21st, 1985, Chris, Jeff, Beth, Linda and a few others headed out for a pleasant day in the country. It was if all present were cognizant that their futures once again held much promise, especially after the ten week ordeal that they had all just experienced. Between hiking and photographing waterfalls, they razzed one another and simply enjoyed each other's company. The school year was ending, and little did they know that this would be the very last time all of them would ever be together in one place again.

The date May 15th, 1985, will be forever engraved in Chris' mind. It was the day the he and Jeff bade goodbye to C2D1.

Above – Chris with Linda and Beth on their final day at Erie Hall: May 15, 1985.

Upon their return to campus the following semester, they both agreed to room as far away from Erie Hall as they possibly could get. Choosing Wayne Hall on the far side of the campus, they spent the remainder of their academic training unmolested by anything paranormal.

Above – "Thirty years later". In 2015, several 1985 Erie Hall residents agreed to be part of a public panel at SUNY Geneseo that discussed the C2D1 Haunting. Also appearing that day was Fr. Charlie Manning, the priest who had blessed room C2D1. Left to right: Paul Davie; Chris Di Cesare; Linda Fox Kalasinski; Craig Norris and J. Jeff Ungar.

THE SURVIVORS

Craig Norris, like many others who have been involved in a violent haunting, for many years he chose to keep quiet about the subject in order to continue to keep his life on track. In October of 2015, at SUNY Geneseo, he publicly shared his recollections of encouraging Chris to continue his running and to end the haunting. Today, he is happily married with two children, is an active outdoorsman, and stays in touch with several of his former college alumni.

Beth Kinsman is married with three children and stated that, for a while, she had intentionally blocked out much of what happened during the Spring semester of 1985. However, in 2012 she agreed to appear on the SyFy show "School Spirits" with Di Cesare and Ungar where she recounted seeing the scratches on Chris' back, her reaction to seeing the picture of the ghost, and about "losing consciousness" while trying to get the ghost to leave her alone.

Linda (Fox) Kalasinski initially denied any knowledge of the haunting, or even recalling several of the participants who were once her friends, regardless of the photographic evidence that showed her involvement otherwise. But as she watched the film 'Please Talk With Me' at the 30th Anniversary Symposium, she began to recall many of the events in quite vivid detail. She is married with two children.

Paul A. who was Chris' original roommate prefers not talk about his experiences during the haunting and has stated that "the past is the past" and that he lives "for the future." In 1994, he did share with researcher Alan Lewis that he left college because the ghost had told him to "leave Chris alone" on several occasions, and that he had witnessed Di Cesare struggling with something invisible for control of his pillow.

Fr. Charlie Manning, now retired, blessed room C2D1 in 1985. He reconnected with Chris and Jeff after hearing Di Cesare mention his name on the "Coast to Coast with George Noory" radio show in 2015. Manning, who spoke at the 30th Anniversary event at Geneseo, recalled the intensity of the students' fear, and sensing that something "powerful" was in their room.

J. Jeff Ungar went on to become a Rare Books Cataloger in Special Collections at the Penn State University Libraries. There, he uses his talents to identify, classify, and conserve ancient manuscripts and books.

Fortunately, a major portion of his own journal notes has survived the years lending written proof that the haunting did in fact occur and preserving an important time line of events during the haunting.

He appeared with Chris on SyFy's "School Spirits", and since the filming of "Please Talk With Me" - the award-winning film which recreates the events of the haunting - the two have rekindled their friendship. In 2015 he married Mara Katria, the film's director.

Chris Di Cesare is a high school history teacher -- is married with two children -- and is well respected in his community.

After the show SyFy "School Spirits – Dorm Room Nightmare" gained national attention, Di Cesare became a fixture on the paranormal convention circuit. His memoir, "Surviving Evidence" (Dark Moon Press, 2014) became an Amazon best seller after an appearance on the "Coast to Coast AM with George Noory".

In October of 1985, he suffered a debilitating injury when a large, but friendly, dog jumped on him during a long distance training session. Knocking him off balance, Chris' foot caught a depression in the road causing his knee to violently twist. While attempting to "run off the pain," he reached the top of a bridge that crossed over a small creek. There he heard a popping sound in his knee, an injury that would bring any Olympic aspirations to an end. Incidentally, the bridge is located next to an historic site where two American Revolutionary Army soldiers were tortured to death in 1779. It is recorded that both captives were ritualistically mutilated and at least one of them had his stomach sliced open, his intestines tied to a sapling and dragged around it until he expired.

The "Torture Tree" is located in Cuylerville, N.Y., and is a stone's throw from the Geneseo State University campus.

The names of the soldiers who lost their lives at the site were Michael Parker and Lt. THOMAS (Tommy) Boyd.

REST IN PEACE

BIBLIOGRAPHY

Spirits of the Great Hill, Mason Winfield, 2001, Western New York Wares, Buffalo, NY

The Iroquois, Dean R. Snow, 1994, Blackwell Publishers, Cambridge, MA.

A Narrative of the Life of Mrs. Mary Jemison, James E. Seaver, reprint - 1995, University of Oklahoma.

Legends of the Longhouse, J.J. Cornplanter, 1998, reprint - Iroqrafts, Ohsweken, Ontario, Canada.

Scalping and Torture, Georg Friederici, 1993, reprint - Iroqrafts, Ohsweken, Ontario, Canada.

History of Livingston County, New York, Edward E. Doty - 1876, J.W.Clement Printer. Geneseo, NY.

The Christopher Di Cesare Interviews, 2012.

The J. Jeff Ungar Interviews, 2012

Wikipedia - Toshihiko Seko

The Demonologist, 1980, Gerald Brittle, Ed Warren, Lorraine Warren, Prentice Hall.

Shadows of the Dark, John Zaffis, Brian McIntyre, 2004, Iuniverse.

ABOUT THE AUTHOR

Timothy T. Shaw

Tim Shaw has had a lifelong fascination with ghosts, the occult and esoteric matters. He is an Ordained Minister, Psychic Medium, Reiki Healer -- achieving the Master/Teacher level, trained Spiritualist Healer, Urban Shaman, Dowser, Paranormal Investigator and Metaphysical Instructor as well as a Historical Interpreter and Backwoods Primitive Weapons Survival Instructor.

PUBLISHED WORKS

As an author, Tim has written *The Ghosts of Buffalo: Spirits, Murder and Mayhem in the Nickel City,* published by Schiffer Publishing. He has also co-authored *Haunted Rochester,* published by History Press as well as *Musings of a Spiritual Wanderer* and *Rev. Zombie's Common Sense Look at the Tools of Divination,* both published by Black Dog Press. Tim has contributed to many other books such as *Animal Spells and Magick* by Marla Brooks and *Cemetery Gates and Haunted Asylums* by Corvis Nocturnum. He has additionally written and published over one-hundred articles in such magazines as *TAPS Para Magazine, Haunted Times, Wilderness Way Magazine, On the Trail,* Camp Chase Gazette, *Military Images, The War Post, The Batavia Daily News, The Fort Niagara Journal* and *Light Bridges.*

Above – The author with C2D1 key witness Chris Di Cesare

For Additional Information about the C2D1 Haunting

Please Talk With Me, 30th Anniversary Edition (CITA Productions, EIA Studios) directed by Mara Katria, is a docu-thriller dedicated to recreating the C2D1 Haunting that occurred at SUNY Geneseo, Erie Hall, Room C2D1 in 1985. To order visit: www.ptwmthefilm.com or www.citaproductions.com

Surviving Evidence, 30th Anniversary Edition (Dark Moon Press) is a first-hand account of the C2D1 Haunting written by Christopher Di Cesare, with Foreword by J. Jeff Ungar and Postscript by William J. Edwards. To order visit: darkmoonpress.com, Amazon.com or the author's website: dicesare.webs.com

Or visit The C2D1 Haunting 30th Anniversary page at: www.c2d1haunting.com

Made in the USA
Middletown, DE
05 January 2019